SAINTS WHO SAW
MARY

OTHER BOOKS BY THE AUTHOR

THE LIFE OF MARY AS SEEN BY THE MYSTICS
MARY COMMUNES WITH THE SAINTS (retitled and republished
as SAINTS WHO SAW MARY)
THE MYSTERY OF THE WIZARD CLIP (booklet)
WORLD SURVEY OF CATHOLIC LEPROSY WORK (booklet)
OUR LADY AND ST. FRANCIS
FIFTY ANIMAL STORIES OF ST. FRANCIS
THE WOUNDED HEART: ST. CHARLES OF SEZZE, FRANCISCAN
BROTHER
FRANCISCAN MYSTIC: THE LIFE OF BLESSED BROTHER GILES OF
ASSISI
TRUE JOY FROM ASSISI: THE ASSISI EXPERIENCE OF INNER PEACE
AND JOY—AN INTRODUCTION TO THE CONTEMPLATIVE
SPIRITUALITY OF ST. FRANCIS
THE ROOTS OF ST. FRANCIS: A POPULAR HISTORY OF THE
CHURCH IN ASSISI AND UMBRIA BEFORE ST. FRANCIS
Co-editor with Ignatius Brady, O.F.M., author of Introduction and
Appendices, and compiler of Bibliography of SAINT FRANCIS
OF ASSISI: A BIOGRAPHY, by Omer Englebert, 2nd English
ed., revised and augmented; translated by Eve Marie Cooper.
Articles in THE NEW CATHOLIC ENCYCLOPEDIA
Articles and Book Reviews in THE CORD and WAY OF ST. FRANCIS.

TRANSLATIONS

THE LITTLE FLOWERS OF ST. FRANCIS
THE PERFECT JOY OF ST. FRANCIS, by Felix Timmermans
THE REVELATIONS OF ST. MARGARET OF CORTONA, by Ange
Marie Hiral, O.F.M.
AN APOSTLE OF TWO WORLDS: GOOD FATHER FREDERIC JANS-
SOONE, O.F.M., by Romain Légaré, O.F.M.

Member of the International Society of Franciscan Studies, Assisi,
and holder of an honorary degree of Doctor of Letters from
St. Bonaventure University, 1982.

SAINTS WHO SAW
MARY

By
Raphael Brown

MEMBER OF THE THIRD ORDER OF ST. FRANCIS
AFFILIATE OF THE FIRST ORDER, O.F.M.

TAN Books
An Imprint of Saint Benedict Press, LLC
Charlotte, North Carolina

Nihil Obstat: Francis J. Reine, S.T.D.
                  Censor Librorum

Imprimatur: ✠ Paul C. Schulte, D.D.
                  Archbishop of Indianapolis
                  April 24, 1954

The Nihil Obstat and Imprimatur are official declarations that a publication contains no doctrinal or moral error. They are not an endorsement of the content or views expressed.

The author wishes to state that in regard to the apparitions, visions, etc., herein mentioned, no claims are made as to their authenticity beyond that which is officially approved by the Church.

Copyright © 1955 by St. Meinrad Archabbey, Inc.

First published in 1955, by St. Meinrad's Archabbey, Inc., as A Grail Publication. Retypeset and republished in 1994 by TAN Books, an Imprint of Saint Benedict Press, LLC. The type in this book is the property of TAN Books, and may not be reproduced in whole or in part, without written permission of the Publisher. (This restriction applies only to reproduction of this *type*, not to quotations from the book.)

Library of Congress Catalog Card No.: 93-61596

ISBN: 978-0-89555-506-9

Cover design by Milo Persic.

Cover image: Our Lady gives the Rosary to St. Dominic and St. Catherine of Siena. From Saint Dominic's Church in the town of Stone, Staffordshire, England. Photo copyright © 2008 by Br. Lawrence, O.P.

Printed and bound in the United States of America.

TAN Books
An Imprint of Saint Benedict Press, LLC
Charlotte, North Carolina

2012

"I have given thee My own most merciful Mother for thine, and it is through her that I will dispense My graces to thee."

—Words of Our Lord
to St. Gertrude (See p. 55).

CONTENTS

FOREWORD

THE CHAPTERS of this book were originally published as a series of articles in *Our Lady of the Cape* magazine. The author herewith expresses his gratitude to the editors of that magazine, the Reverend Oblates of Mary Immaculate, Guardians of the National Canadian Shrine of Our Lady of the Holy Rosary, for permission to reprint the articles in this book.

Each chapter is based on research in the most authoritative and scholarly biographical sources which the writer was able to find in the Library of Congress [where he was employed for 31 years] and in the Catholic University library.

These brief but inspiring glimpses of Our Lady which have been granted to some of the Saints can be considered, as it were, a continuation of the materials compiled in *The Life of Mary as Seen by the Mystics*.

Of course, there are many other saints who have been privileged to see or speak with Our Lady. Many more chapters could have been added to the book, but this would have made for a huge work. Rather, these stories may be considered a small sample of the many wonderful interventions of Mary in the lives of the Saints.

May these mystical communings of the Mother of God with some of her greatest devotees stimulate us, especially in this Marian year [1954], to know and love her better!

SAINTS WHO SAW
MARY

CHAPTER ONE

ST. GREGORY
THE WONDERWORKER
(c. 213-268)

IN THE TOWN of Neocaesarea in Asia Minor during the third century after Christ, there lived a rich and prominent family of pagans whose son, Gregory, was a brilliant and promising young law student. He possessed a keen and inquiring mind, and he relentlessly pursued the truth no matter where it might lead him. Now while he was on a trip to Palestine, Divine Providence, as Gregory himself tells us, led him to meet the fiery Christian philosopher Origen. And when this inspiring teacher had proved to Gregory the necessary limitations of human reason in the most important of all fields of knowledge, namely religion, the young man opened his mind to the light of God's grace and became a fervent and convinced apostle of Christ.

After seven years of study under Origen in the Holy Land, Gregory returned to his home in Neocaesarea. No doubt his friends were shocked to find that this distinguished young man had become a devout, reserved, and humble convert to a mystical other-worldly sect. Certainly Gregory must have

1

been shocked to learn that in all this great and prosperous city, which was steeped in vice and idolatry, *there were exactly seventeen Christians.*

But he was even more disturbed when he heard that the archbishop of the province was planning not only to ordain him a priest, but also to make him a bishop. In his humility Gregory fled into the desert to think over this unexpected summons. Finally he came to realize that God Himself was calling him to share with his pagan neighbors the grace of conversion which God had given him. So he made an agreement with the archbishop that, after a period of spiritual preparation in the solitude of the desert, he would come to be ordained and consecrated.

Now he set about purifying his mind and soul. But he was sorely troubled by one problem. At that time the most bitter controversy was raging over the exact nature of the Holy Trinity, for the language of theology was not so pre-cise then as it has since become. And Gregory also knew that some of the teachings of Origen were not considered orthodox. Consequently, knowing that as a shepherd of souls he would soon have to teach the truth on these difficult subjects, he turned to God and sought divine light in fer-vent and continuous prayer.

One night he fell asleep while still meditating. Then, all of a sudden, a venerable old man with an air of almost superhuman dignity and beauty was standing before him. Gregory jumped to his feet in amazement and asked the stranger, "Who are you? What do you want?"

The old man replied quietly and soothingly, "Calm your-self, my son. I have come to help you."

Somehow Gregory immediately felt reassured, and the other continued in his gentle voice: "God has sent me to enlighten you, to solve the problems that are troubling you, and to teach you the truth you are seeking."

As Gregory was beginning to feel new hope and joy, the stranger raised his hand and pointed to one side.

Looking in that direction, Gregory perceived a dazzling

light, in the midst of which was a woman whose beauty, grace, and majesty were utterly godlike. As he lowered his eyes before this marvelous being, he heard the lovely woman tell the old man, whom she called John the Evangelist, to explain to Gregory the mystery of the Divine Trinity.

Then St. John said, "I will gladly comply with the wish of the Mother of God." And he proceeded to give Gregory an exact and masterful description of the nature of the three Persons who form the Trinity, ending with these words:

"There is therefore nothing created, nothing greater or less in the Trinity, nothing superadded...The Father has never been without the Son, nor the Son without the Spirit; and this same Trinity is immutable and forever unalterable."

In a flash all Gregory's questions were perfectly answered, and he was filled with an inspiring new insight into the deepest mysteries of the Divinity. But now, to his intense sorrow, both the gracious Virgin and St. John vanished from his sight. However, with a prayer of thanks in his heart, he immediately set down in writing the exact words which he had just heard.

And henceforth, as Cardinal Newman writes, he "preached in the Church according to that form, and bequeathed to posterity, as an inheritance, that heavenly teaching." Moreover, Gregory's life was marked by an abundance of miracles. As a result, when Gregory died about thirty years later, he had richly earned his title of St. Gregory "the Wonderworker"—that is, St. Gregory "Thaumaturgus"—and in all the city of Neocaesarea *there were exactly seventeen non-Christians.*

OUR MOTHER OF PERPETUAL HELP. The Mother of God can never be outdone in loving generosity. She appeared to St. Gregory the Wonderworker (c. 213-268), accompanied by St. John the Evangelist, and instructed St. John to explain to Gregory the mystery of the Divine Trinity. In a flash, all of St. Gregory's questions were answered. With thanks in his heart, the Saint wrote down the exact words he had been told.

WITH DIVINE ASSISTANCE, St. Gregory earned the title, St. Gregory "Thaumaturgus," or "The Wonderworker." The Saint is credited with an abundance of miracles. The Blessed Virgin Mary, pictured above as the Sorrowful Mother, inspired St. Gregory to heavenly teaching on the mystery of the Holy Trinity.

CHAPTER TWO

ST. MEINRAD (d. 861) *and* ST. CONRAD OF CONSTANCE (d. 975)

ARLY IN THE ninth century, a saintly, quiet-loving young Benedictine monk named Meinrad, while passing through the city of Zurich on his way to become a teacher at the small monastery of Bollingen, was deeply thrilled when the Abbess-Princess Hildegarde gave him a lovely three-foot wooden statue of the Mother of God holding the Child Jesus in her arms.

Very often during his several years at Bollingen, young Father Meinrad used to gaze out of the window of his cell with ever-increasing longing at a forest-clad mountain on the other side of the lake, for he wished more than anything else to become a hermit and to live a life of prayer, penance and meditation all alone in those woods, like the great hermit-saints of old. Having at last obtained his superiors' permission, one day in the year 828 he took up in his arms his cherished statue of Mary and set out in a wide flat-bottomed boat to cross the lake and become a hermit in the Dark Wood on the slopes of Mount Etzel.

Soon after settling in a solitary retreat he found a nest with two young ravens, which he gladly adopted and tamed, perhaps because the Child Jesus of his statue held a small bird in one hand. Meinrad spent seven years on this mountain, and he was a happy young hermit except for one thing: more and more pilgrims were coming to visit him, attracted by his growing reputation as a saint.

Therefore he fled from his tiny cell, taking his statue and his two friends, the ravens, with him. He went still farther into the depths of the Dark Wood until one day he found, in the midst of the lofty pine trees on a small table-land surrounded by hills on three sides, a bubbling spring giving forth sparkling, fresh mountain water. Here he built himself a little log hut and a chapel, in which he reverently placed Our Lady's statue. His faithful ravens often perched on either side of a crucifix on the gable and watched the holy hermit as he worked and prayed. He was completely happy in this solitude.

But one day a woodcutter discovered Meinrad's retreat, and soon pilgrims were again flocking to receive his blessing and advice. Once some of his Brothers in religion came to visit him, and during the night one of them saw and heard Meinrad reciting his Office with a beautiful seven-year-old boy all dressed in white, who approached the astonished monk and secretly foretold many events which later occurred.

After more than twenty years of prayer and penance, while he was saying Mass in his little chapel on the morning of January 21, 861, the Feast of the Martyr St. Agnes, Meinrad learned by a divine revelation that this was to be his last Mass. With perfect resignation to the will of God, he devoutly received Holy Communion as if it were Holy Viaticum. Then with tears of love in his eyes, the old hermit looked up at his beautiful statue of Mary and begged Our Lady to strengthen him, asking her to offer to her Son the death which he was about to suffer for His glory.

During all the years which Meinrad had spent alone in the Dark Wood, he had never been harmed by the mountain bears or wolves or other wild animals who dwelt there. Now, however, two human beasts of prey, two hardened criminals, hearing that people made pilgrimages to the hermit, were tempted by the idea that he must have precious gifts and rich treasure hidden away in his lonely hermitage. And so this cold winter night they made their way through the deep snow to his retreat in the forest.

Meinrad was just finishing his Mass as they approached, and he now heard the shrill screams of warning of his faithful ravens. With a smile of heavenly joy on his lips, he went out and welcomed the two men with loving kindness and hospitality, setting before them some bread and wine. When they roughly demanded that he show them his hidden treasure, he humbly led them into the little chapel, and pointing to the plain wooden statue above the altar, he said, "I have no other treasure."

Then, with a last loving look at Mary, he folded his hands on his chest, bowed his head, and added calmly, "That for which you have come, do. . ."

In a mad rage the two robbers seized and brutally beat the saintly old hermit to death with a heavy club, while his two ravens flew wildly about, screaming and trying in vain to help their good friend by pecking at the murderers' foreheads.

Then the criminals dragged the Saint's body to his couch of dry leaves in his hut and were about to begin their search for the supposedly hidden treasure when all of a sudden they noticed that a strange yet delicious odor pervaded the place. When they perceived that two candles standing by the hermit's bed had somehow just been lighted without human hand, the two assassins fled in terror all the way to Zurich. But like the accusing finger of God, Meinrad's two ravens persistently followed and attacked the murderers until they were arrested and had confessed the crime.

The body of the holy martyr was taken by his Brothers to the great Abbey of Reichenau near Constance, in which he had entered the Order and been ordained priest.

In the years that followed, pilgrims kept coming to the abandoned little chapel in the Dark Wood, and a few hermit-monks settled there. In the year 906, St. Benno of Strasbourg began to restore and add to the old structures. And in 934, St. Eberhard, also from Strasbourg, arrived and set about building a large monastery and church, the latter enclosing and protecting Meinrad's holy little chapel, which was only eight and a half yards long by six yards wide. When this work was completed in the summer of 948, Eberhard, having become the first Abbot of Einsiedeln, invited St. Conrad, the Bishop of Constance, to consecrate and dedicate the Chapel of Our Lady of the Hermits.

Conrad's party, which included the Bishop of Augsburg and many princes and knights of the Empire, arrived at the hermitage in the Dark Wood on September 13 in the year 948, on the eve of the Feast of the Exaltation of the Holy Cross. And that night there occurred at the Shrine of Our Lady in Einsiedeln one of the most glorious events in all the history of the Catholic Church.

The holy Bishop of Constance retired to his room early in the evening in order to rest after the trip. However, despite his fatigue, he did not fail to get up, as was his custom, before midnight and to go with several religious to pray in the chapel which he was due to consecrate the next morning. While he was fervently beseeching the Blessed Virgin to accept this holy shrine and to make it henceforth a center of pilgrimages where for centuries and centuries she would heal and help her suffering children, suddenly, at exactly midnight, St. Conrad and those with him began to hear the sound of many harmonious voices chanting a melody of heavenly beauty. Looking up, he saw with amazement that the sanctuary of the chapel was filled with a brilliant light that made everything clearer than the brightest noonday sun, and that the altar was completely illuminated

THIS PRECIOUS STATUE of Our Lady of Einsiedeln was placed over the altar of St. Meinrad's simple chapel in the year 828. The Saint had cherished the fond hope of leading a hermit's life, but his solitude was frequently interrupted by visitors who were attracted by his reputation as a saint.

ST. MEINRAD (d. 861), pictured above, and St. Conrad of Constance (d. 975), shown in the fresco below, were both integral to the history of the famous chapel at Einsiedeln, Switzerland. Miraculously dedicated by Our Lord Himself in the year 948, the shrine at Einsiedeln is one of the most popular pilgrimage sites in the world and is visited annually by up to 200,000 pilgrims.

as for a solemn festival. Then he saw coming down from Heaven a magnificent procession of angels under the leadership of St. Michael the Archangel. Some of them formed the choir and were chanting celestial psalms, while others bearing swinging golden censers took their places before the altar.

After the angels came St. Peter with a crozier in his hand, followed by St. Matthew, St. Mark, St. Luke and St. John, who preceded three great Doctors of the Church, St. Gregory, St. Augustine and St. Ambrose. Then came, vested as deacon and subdeacon, the Martyr Saints Lawrence and Stephen. And finally, as High Priest, arrayed in pontifical vestments and wearing a violet chasuble, there appeared in all the splendor of His Divinity, Our Lord and Saviour Jesus Christ. Then, as a breathtaking climax, just before God the Son began the Mass that was to consecrate this holy shrine forever to His Immaculate Mother, Mary herself took her place above the altar of her chapel, radiant with dazzling glory and attended by her train of angelic spirits!

In speechless awe St. Conrad followed every detail of this extraordinary Mass. He observed with rapt attention that the solemn ceremony was performed in the minutest particulars according to the ritual prescribed by the Church for the consecration of a temple, except that at the Sanctus the angels sang: "Holy God, have mercy on us in the court of the Glorious Virgin! Blessed be the Son of Mary who has come to this place and who is to reign world without end!"

More than an hour later, having formally dedicated the shrine to His Blessed Mother under the title of Our Lady of the Hermits, the King of Kings returned in all His majesty to Heaven with His distinguished company of saints and angels. The beautiful living Virgin vanished too, leaving in her place the lovely statue. The singing ceased. The bright light was magically extinguished. And soon the newly consecrated shrine was to all outward appearances exactly as it had been before.

The saintly Bishop of Constance, however, remained kneeling for hours in ecstatic meditation over the marvels which he had just witnessed. Later that morning, when all the dignitaries had assembled and after he had kept them waiting quite a while, he was politely informed that it was time for him to begin the dedication ceremony. Still deeply moved, he firmly declared that the chapel had already been miraculously consecrated by God Himself during the night. But when the Abbot Eberhard and the other officials flatly refused to accept this story and insisted that the ceremony for which so many persons had come together should start at once, St. Conrad yielded. Then another striking supernatural intervention took place: as the Bishop put his foot on the first altar step, the great church was suddenly filled with a strong and impressive voice which everyone present heard exclaim three times:

"Stop! Stop, Brother. The chapel has been divinely consecrated!"

Later on, a full investigation of these extraordinary events was undertaken by the highest civil and ecclesiastical authorities, and in the year 964, in the presence of the Emperor Otto and of St. Conrad, His Holiness Pope Leo VIII issued a bull confirming the miraculous dedication.

It was not long before Einsiedeln became one of the three or four most popular pilgrimage centers in all Europe. For the past nine centuries it has been famous among the Catholic peoples of France, Germany, Austria, Italy and Switzerland as a great and beautifully situated shrine at which Our Lord performs many miracles through the merciful intercession of His compassionate Mother. For several centuries now, over 100,000 — and often as many as 200,000 — devout pilgrims have been visiting Einsiedeln every year. The large church has suffered half a dozen disastrous fires, but not once was Our Lady's little chapel damaged, until the sacking of the shrine during the wars of the French Revolution. The present great basilica and monastery, built in the first half of the 18th century, are one of the most impressive religious monuments in Europe. In 1861 the Benedictine monks solemnly celebrated the 1000th anniversary of the death of their founder, St. Meinrad, whose body had been brought back to his beloved Alpine retreat in 1039, the year in which he was canonized. And on September 14, 1948, Einsiedeln duly marked the 1000th anniversary of the miraculous consecration.

It is deeply significant that, probably in large part due to Our Lady of the Hermits, the sturdy little Christian democracy of Switzerland, whose patron St. Nicholas of Flüe was a hermit and a frequent pilgrim to Einsiedeln, has been able to achieve a hermit-like state of peace and sober well-being amid all the international and civil wars of our times, while participating actively in unselfish brotherly relief and charity work for the unfortunate of all nations. Switzerland has rightly been called the heart of Europe. And the Catholic Canton of Schwyz, in which Einsiedeln is located, is in the heart of Switzerland.

Thanks to Mary, the heart of Europe and the heart of Switzerland have remained a special gateway for receiving graces from Heaven.

CHAPTER THREE

ST. BERNARD OF CLAIRVAUX
(c. 1091-1153)

"MOTHER, PLEASE tell me more about the Knights of Christ!"

A noble young Christian mother was sitting in her home with her young son Bernard, waiting for the church bells to summon them to Matins. It was late on Christmas Eve in the year 1098, in the little school-town of Chatillon in French Burgundy. In order to pass the time and to inspire in her boy the religious vocation which the mother knew by revelation that he was destined to embrace, she had been telling him how the holy old Abbot Robert of Molesmes, with a band of fervent young monks known as the Knights of Christ, had founded in the spring of that year a very strict new monastery at nearby Citeaux.

"He dedicated the house and all his community to the Blessed Virgin," she went on.

"Why?" asked Bernard, a bit sleepily.

"Because he loves her very much and he wants her to protect his work—and also because some time before he

15

was born, she appeared to his good mother and said: 'I want your child to become my spouse!'"

"Oh," murmured little Bernard dreamily, and within a minute he was fast asleep in his mother's arms. And then he had an experience which he never forgot: he saw a lovely young woman praying in a stable—and all of a sudden she was holding in her arms a marvelously radiant baby. Without being told, Bernard recognized the lovable Babe of Bethlehem. Then Mary turned to him and smiled and let him tenderly caress her divine Child...

"Come, Bernard dear," his mother's voice interrupted. "The bells are ringing now!"

Bernard awoke with a start. And on the way to church he excitedly told his mother all about his wonderful vision, which was Mary's Christmas present to both son and mother.

During the thirteen happy years which Bernard spent as a brilliant student at the school of Chatillon, he developed a deep devotion to Mary. He loved to pray and meditate in the church before an old wooden statue of her with her Child on her lap. His ever-growing love for her made him happy, and it made his mother happy, too.

But soon after he left school when he was nineteen, he and his five brothers and one sister lost their beloved and saintly mother. Despite his grief, Bernard felt that henceforth he had two mothers in Heaven.

Now he had to make a big decision: should he become a monk, as he knew his mother had wished, or should he become a great poet, as he himself wished?

He experienced a mystic attraction for the hard life of the holy monks of Our Lady of Citeaux, especially when he prayed to Mary or thought of his mother. He had heard some thrilling stories about the supernatural favors which the Blessed Virgin was showering on that monastery. It was said that the monks knew that she was always present when they were chanting their Office. And once during Office she had appeared to St. Robert's successor, the holy Abbot Alberic, and had given him a dazzling all-white habit as a pattern for the new Order. She had also predicted to a monk that the Order was destined to increase marvelously and to last until the end of the world. And a few years ago, Abbot Alberic had died a beautiful death, his face all aglow, while reciting the words "Holy Mary, pray for us!" in the Litany of the Saints. The present Abbot, an Englishman named Stephen Harding, was also said to have seen Mary in vision.

But all Bernard's relatives vehemently opposed his "burying himself in the woods of Citeaux with those odd monks!" Besides, they insisted, his delicate constitution could never stand such a strict discipline. And then too, Bernard was such a gifted poet! As a matter of fact, he was sorely tempted to go to study in Germany and become a famous writer and scholar.

One autumn day in the year 1111, the handsome youth of twenty-one went into a country chapel, and in deep distress knelt down and begged God to have mercy on him and to help him choose the right way of life. Suddenly he saw his mother—surely Mary had sent her to guide him— and in a flash Bernard knew that God wanted him to become one of Mary's pure, selfless, white-robed monks of Citeaux! In that moment he gladly gave himself completely to God. Henceforth his one rule in life was: All for Jesus through Mary! While warm tears flowed down his cheeks, the young Knight of Christ felt God's healing peace enter and fill his heart.

Bernard was a true apostle: he knew at once that God wanted him to share with others what God had given him. And he did something about it!

The following spring—just when Abbot Stephen was almost despairing of more vocations at Citeaux—Bernard came to the monastery one day and humbly begged permission to enter the Order—with *thirty-one* companions, including several of his brothers and relatives!

Again, Mary and Bernard's mother were happy.

A year later, one of the monks who was especially devoted

ST. BERNARD OF CLAIRVAUX (c. 1091-1153) followed this rule in life: "All for Jesus through Mary." Bernard founded more than sixty monasteries and had such impact on the Church and world in his time that he is said to have "carried the twelfth century on his shoulders."

"TROUBADOUR OF MARY," St. Bernard of Clairvaux was fervently devoted to the Blessed Virgin. It is said that many looked upon him as an angel of God in human form. The Saint's genius shines through in his prodigious writings.

to the Blessed Virgin was granted an inspiring vision of
the Saints in glory in Heaven, including all the Saints of
the Orders of Augustine, Benedict, Cluny, etc. But he was
terribly troubled at not seeing any of his own order. So
he turned in his bewilderment to the lovely Queen of Heaven
and plaintively asked her where were the Cistercians who
loved her so much. With a soothing smile Mary replied,
"The Cistercians are so pleasing to me that, as a hen gathers
her chicks under her wings, so I wish to have under mine
the elect that your order gives to my Son's Kingdom!"

And with a graceful gesture she spread open her great
mantle, revealing to her overjoyed servant on earth a large
number of Cistercian monks and nuns.

Of all these saints, the fiery young Bernard of Clairvaux
soon became by far the greatest in fame. Men everywhere
looked upon him as an angel of God in human form because
of his utterly extraordinary purity, humility, fervor, courage,
justice, charity and eloquence—not to mention the astounding miracles which he performed for years all over Europe.
For after a period of superhuman self-denial and self-
discipline in the cloister, this shy and delicate young poet
was transformed by God's grace and Mary's help into a fearless, energetic, practical Abbot and founder of over sixty
monasteries, an inspired leader of men and reformer of
the Church, to whom Popes, Cardinals, Bishops and Princes
turned for guidance and arbitration. It has even been said
of this true "Superman" of God that "in his solitude he
governed all the churches of the West" and that he "carried
the twelfth century on his shoulders." And yet he found
time to write over four hundred helpful letters, several hundred inspiring sermons, and a number of theological works
of such genius that he is known as "The Last of the Fathers
of the Church" and "The Mellifluous [honey-tongued]
Doctor."

But it is as a loving child of Mary, as the celebrated "Troubadour of Mary," that we are considering St. Bernard at present. His own touchingly fervent devotion to her and his

many moving sermons praising her were so effective in bringing millions of men and women and children to her feet
that some uninformed persons have even stated that he
invented devotion to her, whereas actually all he did was
to spread and increase that devotion, which has been a glorious tradition of the Church ever since the Assumption.

The famous "Memorare" is based on some lines of St.
Bernard. And Cardinal Manning has declared that "of all
the writers of the first thousand years of the Church...none
is more conspicuous for ardent affection and veneration
for the Mother of God."

Three beautiful incidents in his eventful life will now prove
to us both St. Bernard's intense love for Mary and her merciful response to it.

On Christmas Eve in the year 1146, St. Bernard received
a triumphant welcome into the city of Spires. The Emperor
and the Bishop conducted him into the great cathedral and
down the main aisle in solemn procession, while the choir
joyfully sang the beautiful "Hail, Holy Queen." The fifty-six-
year-old Saint no doubt remembered that unforgettable
Christmas Eve vision of his boyhood; and then, recalling
all the marvelous graces and joys which Mary had given
him and through him to countless others during all those
years, as the choir finished with the words "...show unto
us the blessed fruit of thy womb, Jesus," St. Bernard cried
out in a transport of love and gratitude, genuflecting at each
aspiration: "O CLEMENT—O LOVING—O SWEET MARY!"

Though these touching words may have been added to
the prayer earlier, St. Bernard is generally credited with having on this occasion greatly increased their popular use.

Once when gravely ill—during most of his life he suffered
acutely from abdominal pains, because he ate so little—St.
Bernard asked a Brother to pray for him in the chapel. The
humble Brother did so, praying at the altars of the Blessed
Virgin, St. Lawrence and St. Benedict. Meanwhile, Mary and
these two Saints appeared quite clearly before Bernard, who
immediately recognized them with a thrill of joy. Then, smil-

ing down at him in a kind and loving way, they placed their hands gently on the source of his pain—and he was completely and instantaneously cured!

And as a final reward for his long years of faithful service to her Son, when the great Saint died on August 20, 1153 at the age of sixty-three, surrounded by his heartbroken Brothers, Mary is believed to have again appeared to her Troubadour, welcomed his soul when it left his exhausted body and conducted him personally to the throne of his King in Heaven.

"VISION OF ST. BERNARD" by Filippino Lippi (1486) depicts the Blessed Virgin with her hand placed on the Saint's desk.

CHAPTER FOUR

ST. FRANCIS OF ASSISI
(c. 1181-1226)

ONE NIGHT IN July of the year 1216, a small, lean, dark-haired and dark-eyed Italian mendicant friar was fervently praying for humanity in his little thatched hut in the woods. His name was Brother Francis, and even then, though he was only thirty-four, he was known and loved by thousands of persons. Twelve years later, only twenty-two months after his death, Holy Mother Church was to proclaim him St. Francis of Assisi. But in his own eyes, this Poverello, the "Little Poor Man," was "the chief of sinners."

Now, through the silent hours of the night, he implored Almighty God to have mercy on all poor sinners. Remembering Christ's words, "Unless you do penance, you shall all likewise perish," he thought of his own youth. Only twelve years ago he had been a restless, frivolous, ambitious playboy and soldier who hardly gave God a moment of his attention, except on Sunday mornings. And then one night the Lord of Mercy had said to him: "Francis, who can do you most good, the master or the servant?"

23

Francis had taken that great lesson to heart and decided henceforth to put first things first: he asked the Master how he could serve Him. And Jesus Christ Himself, the loving Saviour dying in agony on the Cross for all mankind, had looked down on him with tender affection and said: "REPAIR MY CHURCH!"

Ever since, whenever Francis thought of how kind and good and lovable Jesus was, tears came into his eyes and he exclaimed: "Love is not loved!" At first he had taken Christ's words literally and gladly repaired the chapel in which he had had this unforgettable vision. Then he had come down into these woods on the plain below Assisi, and he had repaired the lovely little old chapel of Our Lady of the Angels, or the Little Portion, "Portiuncula," as it was also called. The peasants insisted that they often heard angels singing above it. And now Francis, as St. Bonaventure tells us, "by reason of the ardent devotion that he had toward the Sovereign Lady of the world...and by reason of his reverence for the Angels...took up his abode there."

It was there that his first Brothers had joined him in a joyful new life of holy poverty, manual labor, caring for leprosy patients, begging, and preaching the love of Christ. And Francis, after renting the chapel from the Benedictine Fathers for a basket of fish each year—for he refused to own anything but his sackcloth habit—and oppressed by the thought of his unworthiness to be the founder of a religious order, had climbed up to a cave in the mountains; there, during a raging storm, he had thrown himself on the ground and with perfect, burning contrition had begged his Saviour to forgive him the sins of his past life. In his anguish of soul he had cried out:

"Who art Thou, my dear Lord and God—and who am I, Thy miserable worm of a servant? My dearest Lord, I want to love Thee! My Lord and my God, I give Thee my heart and my body, and I would wish, if only I knew how, to do still more for the love of Thee!" And he kept repeating: "Lord, have mercy on me, a poor sinner...!"

Then a sweet and gentle peace, the marvelous peace of Christ, came into his pure, penitent soul, and he heard a Voice say: *"FRANCIS, THY SINS ARE WIPED OUT!"*

Ever since, out of heartfelt gratitude, he had been burning with a passionate desire to obtain the same heavenly favor for all repentant sinners. And that was exactly what he was so fervently praying for now, during this summer night, in his hut in the forest near the holy chapel of Our Lady of the Angels...

Suddenly he felt an irresistible impulse to go into the tiny church. Upon entering, as always he knelt, bowed his head and said this prayer:

"We pray to Thee, Lord Jesus Christ, here and in all Thy churches all over the world, and we bless Thee because by Thy Holy Cross Thou hast redeemed the world!"

Then, looking up, to his amazement Francis saw a bright light above the small altar, and in this mysterious radiance he perceived the Redeemer Himself with His Holy Mother and many angels. With keen joy and deep awe, Francis prostrated himself on the floor before this glorious vision, as Jesus said to him: *"FRANCIS, ASK WHAT YOU WANT FOR THE SALVATION OF MEN!"*

Almost overcome at hearing these unexpected words and consumed with seraphic love for His merciful Saviour, Francis exclaimed:

"Though I am but a miserable sinner, I beseech Thee, dear Jesus, to grant this grace to mankind: *Give everyone who comes truly contrite and confessed into this church, complete forgiveness and indulgence of all his sins!*"

Seeing that Christ remained silent, Francis turned with loving confidence to Mary and cried out: "And I beg Thy Blessed Mother, the Advocate of the human race, to intercede with Thee for this request!"

Then Jesus looked at Mary, and Francis was thrilled to see her smile gravely and nod to her Divine Son, as if to say: "Please grant it to him for my sake." At once Our Lord said to Francis: *"I grant your petition. However, you must go to*

My vicar, the Pope, and ask him to approve this indulgence."

Then the wonderful vision vanished, leaving the Little Poor Man sobbing on the ground with relief and gratitude and love. . .

Rising early the next morning, Francis set out with Brother Masseo for the nearby city of Perugia, where a new Pope, Honorius III, had just been elected. But on the way, Francis could not help worrying: after all, he was asking for an unknown chapel, a privilege, such as only the tombs of Christ and Saints Peter and Paul enjoyed! So he prayed and prayed as hard as he could, especially to Our Lady of the Angels.

When his turn came to speak to the Vicar of Christ, Francis said very humbly: "Your Holiness, some years ago I repaired a small church in honor of the Blessed Virgin. I beg you to grant it an indulgence, without offerings." As usual, Francis was thinking of the poor.

The Pope replied: "That is not reasonable, for someone who wants an indulgence should make a sacrifice. But how many years do you wish for this indulgence?"

Knowing very well that plenary indulgences were practically restricted to the Crusades and to St. Peter's, Francis said earnestly: "Holy Father, may it please Your Holiness not to give years, but souls?"

"How do you mean, 'souls'?"

Now he had to come out with it! Sending up a fervent prayer to Our Lady, Francis humbly but firmly voiced his extraordinary request for what was to become known as the "Portiuncula Indulgence":

"I wish, if it please Your Holiness, because of the graces which God grants in that church, that all who go into it, having sincerely repented and confessed and having received absolution, may have all their sins and all punishment for their sins wiped out, both in this world and the next, from the day of their Baptism to the hour when they enter that church!"

Taken aback by such a daring request, the Pope exclaimed: "You are asking for a great thing, Francis, for it is not the custom of the Roman Court to grant such an indulgence. . ."

Realizing that his whole plan to help humanity might utterly fail in another minute, Francis then added quietly, with a burning holy fervor and devastating sincerity: "Most Holy Father, I do not ask you this by myself—*I ask it on behalf of Him who has sent me to you: Our Lord Jesus Christ!*"

In a flash Pope Honorius recalled that his great predecessor, Innocent III, had been utterly convinced that Christ did indeed appear to and guide this remarkable little holy man. And by reports coming in from all over Italy he knew that Francis and his Brothers were indeed repairing Christ's Church by inspiring rich and poor to live pure and simple Christian lives. Therefore, moved by the Holy Ghost, Christ's Vicar solemnly declared three times: *"It is my wish that it be granted to you!"*

But the Cardinals who were present, upon hearing this revolutionary innovation, immediately protested to the Pope, claiming that this rich new indulgence would weaken the Crusades. In the strongest terms they urged him to cancel it. However, the Pope told them: "I will not cancel what I have granted."

"Then restrict it as much as possible," they insisted.

So the Holy Father called Francis back to him and said: "We grant you this indulgence, and it is to be valid for all years in perpetuity—but only for one natural day each year, from vespers on one evening, through the night, until vespers the next evening."

Francis submissively bowed his head, and after thanking the Pope, he rose and began to leave. But the Pope called to him: "Where are you going, you simple fellow? You have no charter yet for this indulgence!"

Francis turned around, and with his charming, trusting smile he said: "Holy Father, your word is enough for me. If this is the work of God, it is for Him to make His work manifest—I need no other document. The Blessed Virgin Mary shall be the charter, Christ the notary, and the angels the witnesses!"

On the way back to their beloved Portiuncula, Francis

ST. FRANCIS OF ASSISI (c. 1181-1226) turned away from a frivolous life and gave himself to the task of "repairing Christ's Church" by saving many souls. Francis was canonized less than two years after his death.

"THE LITTLE POOR MAN." St. Francis of Assisi receives the stigmata in this thirteenth-century rendering attributed to Bonaventura Berlinghieri. The Saint had discarded worldly wealth for the great treasure of holy poverty, imploring God's pardon for his past life with these heartfelt words: "Lord, have mercy on me, a poor sinner."

and Masseo rested awhile. On awaking, Francis prayed, and in his prayer he heard these words: *"Francis, know that this indulgence which has been granted to you on earth has been confirmed in Heaven!"*

With great joy he told his revelation to Brother Masseo, and together they hastened to thank Our Lady of the Angels in her Little Portion.

For the solemn inauguration of this Great Pardon of Portiuncula, Francis chose August 2, because this was the first anniversary of the consecration of the holy chapel, and because August 1 was the Feast of the Liberation of St. Peter from his prison chains. On that day, therefore, in the presence of Bishops from neighboring towns, Francis gave a moving sermon in which he told the people about the Indulgence. Speaking with the love and fervor of an angel on the need for penance and contrition, he exclaimed: "I want to send you all to Heaven!"

Soon afterward, however, seeing the bitter opposition which the Portiuncula Indulgence was arousing among the prelates of the Church, Francis wisely ordered his friars not to publicize the Indulgence further for the time being. To his closest friend, Brother Leo, he said: "Keep it a secret, and do not tell it until near the end of your life. For it is not something for now; this indulgence is to remain hidden for a time. But the Lord will bring it out and manifest it..."

And consequently, none of the early biographers of St. Francis referred to it. But in the 1260's his oldest companion began to talk about it, and after Brother Leo's death in 1271 several witnesses certified that he and his Brothers had told them all about it. Soon the Bishops of Assisi and eventually the Popes issued documents confirming the Great Pardon of Portiuncula, and Mary's tiny chapel became one of the most famous pilgrimage shrines in all Europe.

Later the precious Indulgence was extended to all Franciscan churches throughout the world, and made a *toties quoties* perpetual plenary indulgence applicable to the Poor

Souls in Purgatory. And in 1921 Pope Benedict XV cancelled the one-day restriction at the Portiuncula itself, so that now pilgrims may gain the Great Pardon there on any day of the year. Thus has the Little Poor Man of Assisi enriched the world through his Christlike love for sinners! And his Third Order for men and women in the world, which he called "The Order of Penance," represents the simple, modest, Christian way of life, by means of which millions of humble and penitent and charitable persons have year by year earned the reward of God's true servants. Through the Portiuncula and the Third Order, the Seraphic St. Francis has indeed sent millions of souls to Heaven.

Both Our Lord and the Blessed Virgin have confirmed their approval of the Great Pardon of the Portiuncula. Jesus Christ told St. Bridget of Sweden: *"My Divine Love granted this indulgence to St. Francis that all may be filled with My blessings and receive the remission of their sins."* And once a saintly Franciscan Friar, Blessed Conrad of Offida, saw Mary with the Child Jesus in her arms come down from Heaven in a bright ray of light and stand above the entrance of the Portiuncula Chapel, while the Christ Child with touching affection repeatedly raised His little arm and blessed the pilgrims who were entering His Mother's Little Portion to receive the Great Pardon.

CHAPTER FIVE

THE SEVEN SERVITE SAINTS
(Thirteenth Century)

IN THE YEAR OF OUR LORD 1233, there lived in the thriving city-republic of Florence seven rich, distinguished young businessmen. The youngest of this group of close friends was twenty-seven, and the eldest thirty-five. One was a handsome banker. Another was a scholar. Another was interested in the turbulent politics of the times. Two were married, and one was a widower. All seven were unusually good Catholics. Five years previously they had joined the Confraternity of the Laudesi (Praisers) of Our Lady, and they loved to attend together the regular meetings, at which they prayed and sang hymns in honor of the Blessed Virgin.

Then, all of a sudden, on the Feast of Mary's Assumption, after having received Holy Communion, while they were meditating and making their thanksgiving after Mass, each of these fine young men simultaneously had an unforgettable mystical experience which drastically changed the whole course of his life: each one separately saw a supernaturally bright light, and in it appeared the beautiful Queen of

Heaven, accompanied by many angels. And Mary said to each of them: *"Leave the world and retire together into solitude in order to fight yourselves. Live wholly for God. You will thus experience heavenly consolations. My protection and assistance will never fail you."*

The lovely vision slowly vanished, leaving seven deeply moved young men in the now-deserted church. They looked at one another in stupefied silence, each wondering whether the other had had the same vision, and not knowing whether to reveal what he had experienced. Finally Bonfilius Monaldi, the eldest, took the initiative and humbly told his friends what he had seen and heard. Then the six others excitedly declared they had had exactly the same vision. And soon all seven knelt before the altar and with violently beating hearts resolved to obey this overwhelming divine call.

They went at once to consult the worthy spiritual director of Our Lady's Confraternity, Father James of Poggibonsi. Both he and the Bishop of Florence were so impressed by the young men's sincerity and piety that they approved their decision as fulfilling the will of God. Therefore, during the next three weeks, the seven wealthy businessmen broke the astounding news to their families and friends, who were also inspired by God to acquiesce and cooperate in this extraordinary vocation. It is believed that the two wives entered a religious order. The seven young men sold all their personal property and gave the money to the poor.

At last, on the Feast of the Nativity of Mary, they bade farewell to all their dear ones, exchanged their rich senatorial robes for coarse gray monk's habits, and with the Bishop's blessing they left their comfortable homes and went to live in a dilapidated old farmhouse on the outskirts of the town. While Father James served as their chaplain, they elected Monaldi their superior. However, they had no intention of founding a new religious order. All they wanted was to live an obscure life of extreme mortification and penance and thereby to purify themselves, out of love for God, as His Mother had advised. They spent their time almost entirely in prayer, meditation and penitential exercises, striving in every way to devote themselves completely to Jesus Christ through Mary, in whose honor they reserved every Saturday.

In order to practice humility in one of its most humiliating forms, they asked the Bishop for permission to beg their food from door-to-door among the countless fellow citizens who had known them as prosperous merchants. The Bishop granted them this permission. And as the seven holy friends were passing through the streets, a crowd gathered to watch them. Some considered them cranks, while others felt they were saints. But in this moment a number of babes-in-arms who had never spoken before suddenly cried out: "Look at the Servants of Mary!"

The same thing happened several times later when two of the young men were begging for food. In fact, one five-month-old baby who told his astonished mother to give alms to "the Servants of Mary" grew up to be St. Philip Benizi, one of the most famous Generals of the Order.

But as a result of such sensational events, crowds of visitors began to disturb the holy men's solitude. Therefore they decided to move to some isolated spot far from the city. Not knowing where to go, as usual they turned to Mary for guidance. And in May, 1234, the Blessed Virgin showed them in a vision a lonely tree-covered mountain and said: *"Go to Monte Senario, and live still more austerely!"*

When they consulted the Bishop, they were amazed to learn that this property belonged to the Diocese, and he gladly gave them part of it.

Consequently, early on a beautiful spring morning, after receiving Holy Communion, the seven Servants of Mary joyfully set out in a procession, carrying a large cross and the statue of the Blessed Virgin which had stood in their oratory. As it was the Vigil of the Ascension, they were fasting. They chanted hymns in honor of their Queen as they marched more than ten miles northward through the lovely Tuscan countryside. Soon they caught sight of the mountain of their vision rising above several other hills to an altitude of 2,700 feet. Making their way with the greatest difficulty along an abandoned path overgrown with bushes and brambles, they struggled up through a thick forest of tall pine trees, until at last they came to the mountaintop, where to their great joy they found a beautiful sunlit clearing protected from the wind by the surrounding forest. An opening between the trees provided a marvelous view. It was here that they fixed their cross and knelt to thank Our Lady for guiding them to such an ideal retreat. Then they discovered a spring of sparkling fresh water. And as they filled their lungs with the crisp, cool mountain air, they understood why this height had been named Monte Senario, for "Senario" means "healthy air." Next they set about building a small chapel in the ruins of an old castle, and nearby they put up seven tiny shelters made of boughs, though they had to spend their first nights in caves.

During the following years they led such a strict and mortified life on this mountaintop that once when a Cardinal visited them, he was so shocked by their austerity that he ordered them to be less cruel to themselves. Having observed that some of the seven hermits kept complete silence for long periods, while others persisted in dwelling in caves and tried to live on nothing but herbs, he strongly advised them to adopt one set rule of community life for all.

At the same time they were confronted with another problem: many young men were seeking them out and begging to be admitted into their company. But the seven rejected all such requests, because they still humbly refused to consider themselves a new religious order. So again they turned to Mary for guidance, and consulted their Bishop.

In answer to their fervent prayers, they were given a sign. On the Third Sunday in Lent, February 27, 1239, to their utter amazement they found that a vine which they had planted had miraculously developed green leaves and clusters of ripe fruit, while all around, the other plants remained bare and frostbitten! When this marvel was told to the Bishop, he declared that it had been thus interpreted to him in

(Photos Courtesy of Servite Fathers)

SEVEN DISTINGUISHED YOUNG BUSINESSMEN of Florence, Italy were privileged in 1233 with a vision of the Queen of Heaven accompanied by many angels. The Blessed Mother told each one, "Leave the world and retire together into solitude in order to fight yourselves. Live wholly for God. You will thus experience heavenly consolations. My protection and assistance will never fail you."

THE SERVITE FATHERS received another beautiful visit from the Blessed Virgin, surrounded by angels who bore the habit of the Servite Order as well as a book, a scroll and palms. She promised, "...you will gain these palms in Heaven, if you serve me faithfully on earth."

a dream: the seven branches of the vine represented the seven hermits; the grapes were those who were going to join the Order, for as true religious they were henceforth to spread devotion to Jesus Christ and His Mother among the people.

Accepting this plan as the will of God, the seven holy men decided to reorganize their group on the coming Feast of Easter. Meanwhile they went back to their mountain retreat and prayed more fervently than ever for divine assistance in their new vocation, and they debated among themselves which rule and what sort of habit to adopt.

During Holy Week they redoubled their prayers, fasting, and mortification. Finally, on the evening of Good Friday, April 13, 1239, which that year happened to coincide with the Feast of the Annunciation, while the seven exhausted hermits were saying their night prayers, the Blessed Virgin again appeared to her faithful Servants, surrounded by angels bearing a habit, a book, a scroll and palms. As the holy men gazed at their Heavenly Patroness with rapt devotion, Mary said to them:

"Beloved and elect Servants, I have come to grant your prayers. Here is the habit which I wish you to wear henceforth. It is black that it may always remind you of the keen sorrows which I experienced through my Son's crucifixion and death. This scroll bearing the words 'Servants of Mary' indicates the name by which you are to be known. This book contains the Rule of St. Augustine. By following it you will gain these palms in Heaven, if you serve me faithfully on earth!"

Thus did Mary herself found the new Order of her Servants. She also gave the same message to the Bishop, who gladly erected the group into an order at a beautiful ceremony in their hermitage on Monte Senario. Of the Seven Founders, six now prepared themselves for the priesthood. But one, St. Alexis Falconieri, though he had been a brilliant student, insisted on remaining a simple Brother and servant of the others. Many years later this humble man had the great joy of seeing one of his nieces, Juliana, become a saintly Servite nun.

The new Order of Servants of Mary, or Servite Fathers, expanded marvelously, as the Blessed Virgin inspired many fine young men to join it. Within a few years it numbered over one hundred houses. Mary herself appeared separately to Philip Benizi and Peregrine Laziosi and told them to enlist among her Servants, and both became Servite saints. When the Pope sent St. Peter of Verona to inspect the Order and report as to whether it should be approved or dissolved by the Holy See, Mary appeared to the Saint and told him how dear her Servants were to her.

The Seven Holy Founders, after many years of hard work in her service, were rewarded with particularly beautiful deaths. One passed away while at prayer before the altar, meditating on the sufferings of Our Lord. The first leader and General, St. Bonfilius Monaldi, was in the chapel one morning when he heard Mary's sweet voice say to him: "Good Son, thou hast faithfully listened to and followed the voice of my Son. Come now to receive a hundred times what thou hast given and to possess eternal life!" When another died, a great flame was seen shooting up from his couch toward Heaven. Two more, as tired old men, painfully climbed to their beloved Monte Senario for the last time after long and arduous missionary trips, and passed away at the same moment.

The last to leave this world was the humble Brother, St. Alexis. One day when he was over a hundred years old, knowing his end was near, he paid his last tribute to his Mother in Heaven by reciting a hundred Aves. As he finished, he saw the Child Jesus approach and affectionately crown him with lovely flowers. Then Alexis cried out: "Kneel, my Brethren, do you not see our loving Lord? He will also crown you if, through true devotion to the Blessed Virgin, you imitate her immaculate purity and her profound humility. . ." And thus he went to his reward.

Down through the centuries, the Order founded by these seven loyal Servants of Mary, whom Pope Leo XIII canonized in 1888, has faithfully spread devotion to the Sorrowful

Mother. It was they who gave the Church the beautiful Feast of the Seven Sorrows of the Blessed Virgin Mary. And most significantly it is Mary's Servants, the Servite Fathers, who during recent years of worldwide suffering have been largely responsible for the tremendous, almost miraculous increase in popularity of the Sorrowful Mother Novena.

MONTE SENARIO is the lonely mountain where the Seven Servite Saints were led by the Blessed Virgin. The holy men desired to live an obscure life of extreme mortification and penance, never guessing that they were laying the foundation for the Order of Servants of Mary (Servites), which would become largely responsible for the almost miraculous increase in popularity of the Sorrowful Mother. Novena. The above illustration shows an early seal used by the Saints at Monte Senario.

CHAPTER SIX

ST. SIMON STOCK
(c. 1165-1265)

ALMIGHTY GOD has made His Mother "Mediatrix of All Grace." And it is His will that all men become united in Jesus Christ, her Son. Therefore, as the saintly Pope Pius X declared: "Can anyone fail to see that there is no more direct or surer way (than Mary) to unite all mankind in Christ. . .?"

Now the Blessed Virgin herself has revealed to the world that she wants to draw all humanity under her protecting and sanctifying mantle by means of her Brown Scapular. In two marvelous apparitions, she has solemnly promised us that if we sincerely fulfill the conditions of this beautiful devotion, we shall not only be saved, but she will see that we do not remain long in Purgatory before joining her in Heaven!

For the noble task of giving us her Scapular, Mary selected the great Carmelite Order of contemplative religious, whose sacred tradition of devotion to her goes back to the Old Testament Prophet Elias and to the holy Mount Carmel on which he and his followers dwelt, by the sea, not far from her home in Nazareth.

In the Third Book of *Kings*, we read that when a terrible drought was afflicting Palestine, Elias on Mount Carmel prayed seven times for rain, and at last, "Behold, a little cloud arose out of the seas. . . And behold, the heavens grew dark with clouds and wind, and there fell a great rain . . . And the hand of the Lord was upon Elias." And it has always been a holy tradition in the Order of the Hermit-Brothers of Our Lady of Mount Carmel, which Our Lord Himself has called "The Order of My Mother," that when Elias saw the little cloud, he was shown in a mystical vision a prophetic image of the Virgin who was destined to give to the world the Messias who would save men from the drought of sin. The Prophet therefore instructed his disciples to pray for the coming of this Virgin Mother. And the Carmelite tradition states further that during her life on earth Mary visited the holy mountain near her home, and that after Pentecost the hermits were converted to the Christian Religion, thanks to the prayers of her for whom they had prayed so much.

Ever since, the Carmelites have continued to honor Our Lady and spread devotion to her. In the fourteenth century, the Blessed Virgin appeared to a Carmelite Saint and told him: *"Our Order of Carmel will last until the end of the world, for Elias, the first patron of the Order, asked this of my Son at the Transfiguration and obtained it."*

During the Crusades and the resulting persecution of Christians in the Holy Land, the Hermits of Mount Carmel organized themselves into a religious order and migrated to Europe, where they were welcomed by several rulers who had been greatly edified by their holiness during visits on Mt. Carmel. It was at this time that Mary appeared to the Carmelite, St. Cyril of Jerusalem, and said: *"Carmel is to be a light, not for Syria and Palestine alone — its rays must illumine the entire world!"*

And in the year 1245, when the first General Chapter of the Order in the West was held in Kent, England, the White Friars, as they came to be known, unanimously chose as their General the remarkable Englishman, St. Simon Stock, through whom the Blessed Virgin was soon to give her Scapular to the world.

Even as a child, St. Simon had an unusually intense devotion to Mary. While still in his teens, he became a hermit and lived in the hollow trunk of a great tree. A small dog used to bring him crusts of bread. And young Simon used to make pilgrimages to shrines of Our Lady. To honor her, he would compose poems about her and carve her name on trees. Often she appeared to him in visions, and guided and advised him. And once she revealed to him that in a few years some holy hermits would come from Mt. Carmel, and that he should join their Order, which was especially dedicated to her service.

Having met some of the Brothers of Carmel, Simon studied for the priesthood and was ordained at the age of forty. Then he made a pilgrimage to the Shrines of the Holy Land and remained for several years with the hermits on the Mount, living their strict penitential life of silence and contemplation. Later he returned to Europe as a full-fledged Carmelite apostle and devoted himself to establishing the Order in the West.

However, after his election as General, the Saint found the task of organizing a group of contemplative hermits into an order of mendicant friars in Europe almost beyond his capacities. And so, when disruption and ruin threatened his beloved Order in the summer of 1251, the aged St. Simon Stock withdrew to his monastic cell and begged the Heavenly Patroness of the Brothers of Carmel to help her children in their hour of need.

Throughout the night of July 15, St. Simon prayed on his knees to Our Lady of Carmel. And remembering his custom as a youth of greeting her in verse, he poured forth with many tears the love and anguish of his noble heart in these beautiful lines:

Mary Magazine, Aylesford (Darien, Ill.)

ST. SIMON STOCK after receiving the Carmelite Scapular (Brown Scapular) from Our Lady. She said to him, "Receive, my beloved son, this habit of thy Order. This shall be to thee and to all Carmelites a privilege, that whosoever dies clothed in it shall not suffer eternal fire."

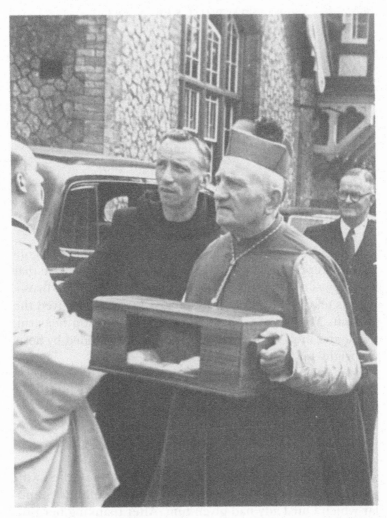

THE SKULL of St. Simon Stock was translated to Aylesford, England in 1951 (pictured above). The remainder of the Saint's body remains at Bordeaux, France, where he died in 1265 while making a visitation to the Carmelite foundation there.

Flos Carmeli,	Flower of Carmel,
Vitis florigera,	Blossom-laden vine,
Splendor coeli,	Splendor of Heaven,
Virgo puerpera,	Virgin-Mother
Singularis!	Unique!
Mater mitis,	Tender Mother,
Sed viri nescia,	Yet Virgin too,
Carmelitis	To the Carmelites
Da privilegia!	Grant favors!
Stella Maris!	O Star of the Sea!

Suddenly, toward dawn, as the Saint was humbly and confidently repeating this fervent prayer, he became aware that his cell was filling with a marvelous supernatural light. Brushing his tears from his eyes, he looked up and perceived the glorious Mother of God with the Infant Jesus on her arm, living and moving in dazzling splendor, surrounded by hosts of bright angels!

Our Lady of Mount Carmel held in her hand a large Brown Scapular with a square opening for the head. Giving it to her astounded servant, she said:

"Receive, my beloved Son, this habit of thy Order: This shall be to thee and to all Carmelites a privilege, that whosoever dies clothed in it shall not suffer eternal fire!"

As Mary and the Child vanished, the Saint was filled with joy and gratitude on seeing himself clothed with the Scapular which Our Lady had given him. After thanking her profusely for this great gift, this garment of grace, and for her marvelous promise (which can be called a guarantee of either final perseverance or of final repentance, whichever is needed), he hastened to assemble his brethren and tell them what had happened.

Thus did the Blessed Virgin grant to the Carmelites a favor that saved the Order. The following January, the Pope and the King of England issued letters of protection and favor for the Carmelite Order. Soon Mary's Scapular was officially adopted as the regular habit of the White Friars. And the Scapular devotion with its saving Promise began to spread throughout Europe, as the Carmelite Fathers established Scapular Confraternities, whose lay members were given scapulars—abbreviated versions of the Scapular of the Carmelite habit. By being "enrolled" in the Brown Scapular, a person becomes enrolled in the Scapular Confraternity, which is attached to the Carmelite Order. In 1276, fifteen years after St. Simon Stock's death, Pope Gregory X died wearing a small scapular, which was found incorrupt when his tomb was opened in 1830.

In time, Mary's Brown Scapular became one of the most popular Catholic devotions. A historian has written: ". . .there was no invocation more honored in all Christianity than that of Our Lady of Mount Carmel. At the period when St. Bernadette lived, in all Christian families most children wore the Brown Scapular on their breast." Pope Pius XI declared: "I learned to love the Scapular Virgin in the arms of my mother." When Pope Leo XIII felt death approaching, he said: "Let us make a novena to Our Lady of the Scapular, and I shall be ready to die!" This is the devotion concerning which a learned Jesuit writes in the *Catholic Encyclopedia:* "Like the Rosary, this Scapular has become the badge of the devout Catholic and the true servant of Mary."

CHAPTER SEVEN

ST. MECHTILDE
(c. 1240-1298)

THE LIVES OF St. Mechtilde and St. Gertrude the Great seem to have been one long series of visions and conversations with Our Lord and His Mother, whom they loved and served in the Cistercian convent of Helfta in central Germany during the second half of the thirteenth century. At the express command of Christ Himself, despite all the humble objections of the two Saints, their beautiful revelations were carefully recorded in two precious books, *The Book of Special Grace* of St. Mechtilde and *The Herald of Divine Love* of St. Gertrude, in order that "in the far future," as Jesus said to the latter, "these writings may be a pledge of My divine bounty. . .through them I will benefit innumerable souls."

St. Mechtilde was born about the year 1240, a countess and a cousin of the Emperor. But at the age of seven she entered a convent school and henceforth lived only for the King of Kings. She soon became an unusually learned nun, capable of writing elegantly in Latin, and she had such a lovely voice that she was made choir mistress of her convent and became known as the Nightingale of Christ. But above all she excelled in pure, ardent, soaring devotion to her beloved Saviour and His glorious Mother.

One day she begged Our Lord to teach her how to greet the Blessed Virgin, and He then gave her this touching tribute to the Immaculate Heart of Mary:

"If you wish to please My Mother, hail her virginal heart in the abundance of all the good things of which it is an abyss for mortals. Hail that heart in its purity, which inspired Mary to take the hitherto unprecedented vow of perpetual virginity. Hail it in its humility, which most of all made her find grace before God and made her worthy of conceiving by the Holy Spirit. Hail it in its ardent longing, by which she had the power of drawing Me into her womb. Hail it in its great charity for God and men. Hail it in its extreme fidelity in keeping grace and in remembering all that I did and said during My childhood and all My life. Hail it in the compassion with which she shared in all My sufferings, which cruelly pierced and tore her soul. Hail it in her submission to the will of God, that submission by which she consented to sacrifice Me, her only beloved Son, for the salvation of the world. Hail it in the very motherly solicitude with which she unceasingly prayed for the infant Church. And finally, hail it in her continuous prayers by which, through her merits, she obtains for human beings all the graces which are given to them."

On another occasion, when the Mother of God herself appeared to Mechtilde, the Saint asked her how she could honor her, and Mary replied:

"Remind me of the joy which I experienced when the Son of God left the bosom of His Father in order to come into my womb. Congratulate me again on the ineffable bliss with which I was filled when that same Son was born of me, and when I saw Him and pressed Him in my arms as a mother."

ST. MECHTILDE OF HELFTA, Germany. A Latin inscription beneath the original picture is translated thus: "Saint Mechtilde of Helfta, Virgin, of the Order of St. Benedict, the great sister of the Great and Admirable Gertrude, insofar as she was most enlightened by revelations and divine gifts. She was consecrated to God when she was hardly born, to be espoused to Christ rather than to the world. She received the Heart of Jesus, giving It back in death, having been promised the certain reward of beatitude. At her death, she was invited by Jesus in these words: 'Come, blessed one.'"

OUR LADY OF ALTÖTTING, Germany. This statue, which dates back to the thirteenth century, testifies to the long-standing Marian devotion of Catholics in Germany.

One Saturday, during a Mass in Our Lady's honor, Mechtilde exclaimed: "O most gracious Queen of Heaven, I would love to greet you with the most pleasing salutation which has ever been addressed to you!"

At once Mary appeared to her with these words written on her Immaculate Heart in letters of gold: "HAIL MARY, FULL OF GRACE! THE LORD IS WITH THEE!" And she said to the Saint: "No creature has ever said anything that was more pleasing to me, nor will anyone ever be able to find or say to me anything that pleases me more."

One day when Mechtilde was reproaching herself for not having loved the Blessed Virgin enough, Jesus appeared to her and said:

"For this fault, and in order to make reparation for it, first praise and honor My Mother for the faithfulness with which, in all her actions and throughout her life, she submitted her will to Mine; secondly, praise and honor the readiness with which she attended to all My physical needs and with which she had compassion in her heart for all that I had to endure with My body; and thirdly, exalt her for devotion to Me in Heaven, by means of which she draws sinners to Me, converts them to Me, and frees from the sufferings and flames of Purgatory a multitude of souls, for whom her intercession and her powerful intervention more quickly open the realms where they will glorify Me for all eternity."

Once when Mechtilde had committed some slight fault, Our Lady showed herself to the Saint with a stern face and threatened her with a golden whip, lest the nun repeat her fault. However, the Saint was given to understand that the gold of the whip symbolized Mary's kindness and love. In this connection also, Mechtilde once heard Jesus say to Mary: "Remember, My beloved Mother, that for your sake I am indulgent to sinners, and I regard my elect (Mechtilde) as if she had served you all her life with devotion." Whereupon Mary lovingly gave herself entirely to the Saint, for Jesus' sake.

During Mass on a Feast of the Assumption, Mechtilde had the following vision: she beheld the Blessed Virgin extending her mantle as if to receive beneath its shelter all those who fled to her patronage. Then the holy Angels brought and presented to her, as fair young virgins to their mother, all who had prepared themselves very fervently for this Feast, meanwhile protecting them from evil spirits and inciting them to good deeds. Then there appeared a num-ber of little animals, representing sinners who devoutly pray to Mary, and she received them with great charity and covered them too with her mantle. At the Elevation, Our Divine Lord Himself blessed all who assisted at Mass with special devo-tion toward His Mother in her glorious Assumption, so that they were strengthened in their good desires.

When Mechtilde was dying, she prayed very earnestly to Mary for the nuns of her community, and the Blessed Vir-gin took the Saint's hand in hers, indicating that she accepted from her the charge of the convent. Then Our Lord placed on Mechtilde a necklace of marvelous beauty, sparkling with gems.

CHAPTER EIGHT

ST. GERTRUDE
(c. 1256-c. 1302)

A FTER ST. MECHTILDE'S holy death, Jesus made this revela-
tion to another nun: "I have done great things in
Mechtilde; but I will accomplish still greater things in
Gertrude."

St. Gertrude the Great, the famous forerunner of St. Margaret Mary in devotion to the Sacred Heart, had entered
the convent school as a five-year-old orphan. There little
"Truda," in her miniature nun's habit, was trained in knowledge and sanctity by St. Mechtilde. Gertrude too was a brilliant student. In fact, she later repented for having studied
so much during her youth that she neglected her prayers.
At the age of twenty-five, her heart was filled with an
indescribable longing and unrest, and she began to feel disgust for the vanity and curiosity which pride had raised
in her soul despite her being a religious.

Then on January 27, 1281, as she later wrote, "just at the
beautiful hour of twilight, raising my head, whom should
I behold but Thyself, O my Beloved, my Redeemer! Thou

didst appear to me as a lovable, modest youth of sixteen years of age. Standing before me, Thou didst say, in an indescribably sweet tone: 'Thy salvation is near at hand...I will save thee...With My enemies thou hast liked the earth...Return to Me. I will welcome thee tenderly.' ...And now, from this moment, my soul was enlightened, my heart softened, Thy powerful grace extinguishing within me all inordinate passion for worldly reading and detaching me from all my vanities, so that I came to sacrifice those things which formerly attracted me, Thou alone being pleasing to my soul."

Thereafter for twenty years Our Lord appeared to Gertrude at least once every day, except for a period of eleven days when He withdrew in punishment for a worldly conversation. Very often He urged her, as His Church urges us all, to come to Him through Mary.

When Gertrude asked Him what she could do to please Him more, Jesus answered: "Behold My Mother. Endeavor to praise her worthily." In the early years of her conversion, Our Lord said to the Saint: "I give thee My sweet Mother as thy Protectress. I confide thee to her care." And when during a trial Gertrude called upon Jesus to help her, He replied: "I have given thee My own most merciful Mother for thine, and it is through her that I will dispense My graces to thee." Henceforth Gertrude always begged Mary to prepare her for her Communions, during which the Saviour often appeared to her and consoled her.

Once, as the Saint was praying to Jesus to offer His Mother something to make up for her own lack of devotion toward the Blessed Virgin, Our Lord arose, and offering Mary His Sacred Heart, He said:

"Most loving Mother, behold My Heart. I offer it to thee with all that divine and eternal Love which prompted Me to choose thee for My Mother. In this Heart I offer thee all that filial affection of which I gave thee so many tokens on earth, when thou didst nourish and carry Me as a little child in thy arms. In this Heart I offer thee that faithful

ST. GERTRUDE THE GREAT, orphaned as a child, was taught in a convent school by St. Mechtilde. St. Gertrude was told by Our Lord, "I have given thee My own most merciful Mother for thine, and it is through her that I will dispense My graces to thee." In one particular vision, St. Gertrude saw Our Lord offer His Sacred Heart to His most Blessed Mother. St. Gertrude is known as a forerunner of St. Margaret Mary in devotion to the Sacred Heart.

EVEN DURING HER LIFETIME, the sublime sanctity of St. Gertrude was revealed to many souls by Our Lord Himself. Jesus told St. Mechtilde, "I have united My Heart so closely to Gertrude's soul by the ties of My mercy that she has become one spirit with Me."

love which kept Me near thee all My mortal life, obedient
to thy wishes, as any other son to his mother. I offer thee
especially that love which on the Cross made Me in a measure forget My tortures to compassionate thy bitter desola-
tion and to leave thee in My place a guardian and son.
And lastly, behold in My Heart the love which prompted
Me to exalt thee in thy blessed Assumption far above the
Saints and Angels and to crown thee Queen of Heaven and
earth."

And on a similar occasion, Gertrude saw Jesus go up to
His Mother with the greatest respect, kneel down before
her and, bowing His head, greet her in a most gracious
and tender manner.

Once when Gertrude prayed to Mary to fill her heart with
such virtues that God would take pleasure in dwelling in
it, Our Lady stooped down and planted in the Saint's heart
various symbolic flowers: the rose of charity, the lily of purity,
the violet of humility, the sunflower of obedience and many
others, showing thereby how promptly she assists those who
invoke her.

The following day the lovely Mother of God appeared
to Gertrude, in the presence of the Blessed Trinity, under
the form of a dazzling white lily with three splendid leaves.
Mary said to the Saint: "If anyone greets me devoutly as
the white Lily of the Trinity, the brilliant Rose of Paradise,
I will do for him what I can through the Omnipotence of
the Father, the Wisdom of the Son, and the superabundant
mercy which fills my heart, flowing from the Love of the
Holy Spirit."

From that day Gertrude frequently greeted Mary with this
prayer:

"I hail thee, white Lily of the glorious and ever peaceful
Trinity, brilliant Rose, delight of Paradise, of whom the King
of Heaven wished to be born, and with whose milk He wished
to be nourished. Nourish our souls with divine graces!"

The Blessed Virgin Mary rewarded Gertrude's fervent devotion on one Feast of the Assumption when she rose from

her throne in Heaven and beckoned Gertrude to come and take her place. But Gertrude drew back, exclaiming: "O Queen of glory, what can I do to merit so great a favor?" Then Our Lady explained that she could use her merits, especially Mary's purity, humility and charity, and offer them to God to obtain this privilege. Thus clothed in Mary's merits the Saint received her Lord in Holy Communion. Finally, in a marvelous vision she saw the glorious Mother of God conducted up to highest Heaven by her Divine Son amid the rejoicing of all the Saints and Angels. Then with her Son's right hand, Mary blessed Gertrude's convent, and the nun saw a gold cross shine over each of her sisters' heads.

The last of Mary's many touching favors to St. Gertrude occurred at the latter's death: brilliant with splendor, the merciful Virgin came to console her loving handmaid, and bending down, she gently and affectionately supported the dying Saint's head, as the King of Glory with infinite tenderness inclined toward His faithful servant and drew her beautiful soul to Himself forever.

CHAPTER NINE

ST. BRIDGET OF SWEDEN
(c. 1302-1373)

O F ALL THE SAINTS in the history of the Church, it would
seem that none ever enjoyed more frequent intimate
talks with Our Lord and His Blessed Mother than the great,
yet insufficiently known, St. Bridget (or Birgitta) of Sweden,
to whom the Saviour said: "You are to be My spouse and
My channel."

Of which other saints can it be recorded that, besides
a long life filled with holy example, miracles and practical
reforming action, they also gave to the world over 650 revelations which have received the admiring approval of the
Church? These extraordinarily rich *Revelations of St. Bridget*
contain many lengthy, inspiring and enlightening discus-
sions by Our Lord and His Mother on such important subjects as the Church, moral advice for clergy and laity,
marriage and education, wealth and voluntary poverty; eighty
pages for rulers on Christian principles of statecraft and
war; messages from St. Ann, St. John the Baptist, St. Matthew, St. Agnes, St. Francis of Assisi; many instructive

instances of conditions in Purgatory; a complete rule for a new religious order, including minute details as to conventual life, liturgy and architecture, dictated by Christ Himself; a series of beautiful prayers and lessons for the Divine Office revealed by an angel; and finally, many valuable accounts of events in the lives of Jesus and Mary (which were included in *The Life of Mary as Seen by the Mystics*). And yet all these God-given treasures of divine wisdom, although fully approved by several Popes, have unfortunately been allowed to fall into an unjustifiable neglect: apart from an out-of-print German edition of 1888, the complete *Revelations of St. Bridget* are not available today in any modern language except Swedish. However, during the recent war [World War II], the great Danish Catholic writer Johannes Joergensen crowned his distinguished career with a splendid two-volume biography of the Scandinavian Saint, which was subsequently published in English. But it is strongly to be hoped that St. Bridget's marvelous *Revelations* will also soon become available.* That Our Lord wishes them to be known and appreciated by modern Christians too can be deduced from the following words which He spoke to His "channel," Bridget:

"Know that I do not speak to you for your own sake only, but also for the salvation of all Christians. . . Know also that when it pleases Me, men shall come who will take up the words of the divine *Revelations* with joy and consolation. . . My words, which you often hear in spiritual visions, like a wholesome drink satisfy those who thirst for true love, give warmth to the cold, cheer the sorrowful and heal those whose souls are sick."

One night, when Bridget was a mere child of eight, she woke up and saw a beautiful altar on which was sitting a lovely lady in shining white clothes, holding a gleaming crown

---

* Cf. the small book of selections therefrom published under the title *Revelations of St. Bridget—On the Life and Passion of Our Lord and the Life of His Blessed Mother* (TAN, 1984). —*Editor,* 1994.

in her hands. "Come, Bridget," said the lady. Recognizing her as Mary, little Bridget sprang out of bed and knelt at her feet. "Do you want to have this crown?" the Virgin asked, and as the girl eagerly nodded, she saw and distinctly felt Our Lady gently place it on her head. Many years later St. Bridget stated that she could never forget this decisive experience, for it made her understand that she was to live her life as a burning sacrifice of love for God in return for the crown of eternal life.

A few years later, while praying one evening before a crucifix, Bridget suddenly saw the living Christ bleeding on the Cross and heard Him say: "See how I am wounded!" Stricken with horror by the vividness of His suffering, the ten-year-old Bridget exclaimed: "O Lord, who did that to You?" And the dying Saviour replied: "Those who scorn Me and neglect My Love."

After losing her mother while still a young girl, Bridget often turned to the merciful Mother of God for help. Once when she had a particularly difficult piece of embroidery to do, she begged Mary to assist her; and one of Bridget's cousins, coming into the room, saw bending over her and directing her work a beautiful lady—who suddenly vanished!

At the age of fourteen Bridget was obliged by her family to marry. But God gave her an unusually devout young husband named Ulf (or Wulf), with whom she lived in deep spiritual harmony and pure Christian happiness for twenty-eight years. This model young Christian couple trained themselves in chastity and continence, and they prayed to God to give them only children who would serve Him well. In this connection Our Lady later said to Bridget:

"Hear me, you who pray to God with all your heart that your children may please Him. Truly, such a prayer is pleasing to God. And there is no mother who loves My Son more than anything on earth and who prays for this grace for her children whom I would not be ready to help at once to fulfill her prayer. Also, there is no widow who faithfully prays for help to remain a widow until death, in order to honor God, whose wish I would not be ready to fulfill at once, for I too was like a widow, as on earth I had a son who had no physical father. Also there is no young woman who prays to God to keep her virginity until death whom I would not be ready to protect and to strengthen, because I am truly a Virgin myself."

Once when Bridget was suffering in childbirth, a mysterious lady was seen standing by her bed and relieving her pains. Later, Mary reminded Bridget of this help, saying: "When you had trouble in childbirth, I, Mary, came to you. So you would be ungrateful if you did not love me. Therefore, strive that your children may be mine, too. The daughter of Joachim, who is the Mother of God, wishes to be like a mother to the children of Ulf and Birgitta."

At the age of forty-five, Bridget's devout husband entered a Cistercian monastery, and died a year later. Soon after she became a widow, when her five grown children were all either married or provided for, Bridget, who had for many years been leading the life of a saintly member of the Third Order of St. Francis, gave herself entirely to God. Then, in 1346, that wonderful series of mystical experiences and conversations began which her confessors carefully recorded in the nine Books of her *Revelations*.

One day the glorious Mother of God appeared to Bridget and said: "I am Mary, the Queen of Heaven and the Queen of Angels. My Son loves you with His whole heart; therefore love Him, too. When you have Him, you have all virtues."

Later Our Lord accepted Bridget as His mystical Spouse, and then His sweet Mother said to her: "As my Son has given you the name of His new Spouse, so I now call you my Daughter-in-Law. For God and I want to show our will to our friends in the world through you."

When personally training Bridget in sanctity, the Blessed Virgin often instructed her on such varied subjects as modesty in dress, dancing and various ways of practicing true Christian wisdom and humility. For her future work in correcting and converting extraordinary sinners, Bridget

ST. BRIDGET OF SWEDEN (c. 1302-1373) is depicted here in front of a crucifix, reminding us of her many visions of Our Lord and His Mother. The Saint was personally trained in sanctity by the Blessed Virgin, who told her, "Meditate on my sorrows and my tears, and mourn that the friends of God are so few."

OUR LORD communicates a message to St. Bridget. When Our Lord accepted Bridget as His mystical Spouse, Our Lady said to her, "As my Son has given you the name of His new Spouse, so now I call you my Daughter-in-Law. For God and I want to show our will to our friends in the world through you."

was shown in case after case how great God's mercy and how powerful Mary's intercession for them are, if only they ask for it. Once Mary told Bridget:

"I am the Mother of Mercy, the joy of the just, and the gate to God for sinners. In the fire of Purgatory there is no suffering that through my intercession would not be more easily bearable than otherwise. No one is so damned that, as long as he lives, he will lack my mercy. No one is so far from God, if he is not completely accursed, that he may not come back to God and obtain mercy when he appeals to me."

The Sorrowful Mother of the Crucified Saviour also explained to Bridget that her Immaculate Heart was so full of compassion for the sufferings of sinning humans because she had herself suffered so much from their sins: "From my Son's birth until His death, I was filled with grief. Tears used to come into my eyes when I gazed at His hands and feet, which the nails were going to pierce. . .when I meditated on His future Passion. . .and when I saw the Prophets' sayings concerning Him all being fulfilled. . .And now I look at all the human beings on earth to see whether maybe there are a few who feel compassion for me and who think of my sorrows, but I find very few who meditate on my suffering and sorrows. Therefore, my daughter, do not forget me, for I am forgotten and ignored by many. See my grief, and imitate me as well as you can. Meditate on my sorrows and my tears, and mourn that the friends of God are so few. . .I am grieved over the enemies of my Son in the world who now crucify Him worse than the Jews formerly did. With their vices they crucify my Son in a spiritual way more cruelly and more fearfully than those who crucified Him physically."

Because many of these enemies of Our Lord were Christians, in the year 1350 the King of Kings sent His humble Swedish servant to Italy to reprove and convert certain princes and rulers, monks and prelates, with forceful warnings that unless they changed their way of living, they would soon suffer grievous punishments—which did invariably overtake those who refused to reform. Through her He also transmitted several messages to His Vicar in Avignon, France (where the Popes resided for some seventy years), bidding him to return to Rome. And once Our Lord pointed out to Bridget a section of the city of Rome around St. Peter's Basilica and told her that one day "a Pope who loved the Church as much as did He Himself and His friends would possess that place in peace. . . " This striking but little-known prophecy apparently came true more than 550 years later with the creation of Vatican City in 1929.

Finally, after thirty-three years of regenerating and miracle-working holiness of life in Rome, and after a fruitful pilgrimage to the Shrines of Jerusalem and Bethlehem, the famous Scandinavian Saint suffered a painful and prolonged illness. Before she died, however, the Blessed Virgin appeared one last time to her beloved "Daughter-in-law" and said:

"You are going to give life to strong and healthy children devoted to God. . .Blessed Francis too was sick for a long time. . .You may ask why your illness has lasted so very long. . .I answer you—that my Son and I love you. When my Son told you as you entered the Church of His Holy Sepulcher that all your sins were forgiven, He did not say that you would not suffer any more during the rest of your life on earth. For it is the will of God that the love of men should correspond to the love of God, and that earlier negligences should be expiated in patience and sickness. . .Do not the doctors say that you are not dying? Truly, my Daughter, they do not pay attention to what death means: for that man dies who cuts himself off from God and becomes hardened in sin. And he who does not believe in God and who does not love his Creator is also dead. But whoever fears God at all times and cleanses himself from his sins through frequent Confession—whoever yearns for union with his God has life and shall not die!"

A PRAYER TO MARY
REVEALED TO ST. BRIDGET

"Rejoice, O Lady, Virgin Mary, in that, in the glory of Heaven, thou knowest thyself to be both a Mother and a Virgin, free from every stain of sin — nay, adorned with so many actions done out of purest love that thou fully under-standest that God's justice owes thee the very highest honor. Then didst thou also understand that whosoever shall have loved God most ardently in this world shall have his place nearest to Him in Heaven...

"Be thou blessed, O my Lady, Virgin Mary, in that every faithful soul praises the Holy Trinity because thou art its noblest creation, an ever ready intercessor on behalf of souls in need and the Advocate and most trusted Protectress of all sinners. Praise, therefore, be to God the Sovereign Emperor and Lord, who has so exalted thee that thou art also Empress and Lady in the everlasting Kingdom, reign-ing with Him, world without end. Amen."

ST. BRIDGET OF SWEDEN TENDERLY HOLDS an image of the Blessed Virgin and the Infant Jesus. When only eight years old, the Saint awoke one day to see the Blessed Virgin seated upon a beautiful altar. Our Lady gently placed a gleaming crown on St. Bridget's head, from which the little girl understood that she was to live her life as a burning sacrifice of love for God in return for the crown of eternal life.

CHAPTER TEN

ST. CATHERINE OF SIENA
(1347-1380)

O N THE FEAST of the Annunciation in the year 1347 there was born in Siena, "the City of the Virgin," a young woman of extraordinary charm and will power who, in only thirty-three years of heroic sanctity in action, lived and suffered and died for the Mystical Body of her beloved Lord and is known to history as St. Catherine of Siena, one of the greatest of all the Church's saints—and one of the most fascinating.

During her short span of life she personally converted to sincere Christian living so many men and women of all ages and classes that her friends knew that all they had to do was just to introduce the sinner to her, and then, by the simple magic of God's holy charity in Catherine's heart and personality, henceforth that person would become another "Caterinato," as the Sienese called the members of her numerous "family" of enthusiastic friends and followers.

Catherine was so utterly devoted to her Saviour that He is the center of nearly all her many mystical experiences, and consequently His humble Mother plays a less visible part in the life of this Spouse of her Divine Son. However, as we shall see, the Saint had a very loving and confident devotion to the sweet Mother of God, and in a number of significant incidents in her life it was to Mary that she turned or it was Mary who came to her aid.

As a young child of the City of the Virgin, little Catherine soon began to pray to the lovely Queen of Siena, and often she was heard hailing Mary on each step as she went up and down the stairs in her home. Then one day while walking along a street with her brother—she was only six years old—she looked up and suddenly saw above the roof of St. Dominic's Church the King of Kings on a splendid throne, dressed as the Pope with the papal crown on His head; and with Him were St. Peter, St. Paul and St. John. Looking down at young Catherine with tender love, Christ slowly and solemnly gave her His blessing, making the Sign of the Cross over her with His right hand three times, like a bishop.

From that moment Catherine was no longer a child. She had fallen in love—forever—with her loving Saviour. According to one of her contemporary biographers, "That vision and that blessing were so mighty that she could not think of anything but the holy hermits and of imitating them."

The following year, therefore, before a picture of Our Lady, she promised herself to the Lord who had thus blessed her. In this crucial moment she prayed to Mary:

"Most blessed and most holy Virgin, look not upon my weakness, but grant me the grace that I may have for bridegroom Him whom I love with all my soul, thy most holy Son, our only Lord, Jesus Christ! I promise Him and thee that I will never have any other bridegroom."

Consequently, when Catherine was thirteen and her family wanted to force her to marry, after consulting a Dominican Father about her vow she simply cut off all her fair hair! And as her parents then prevented her from praying so much in solitude by overworking and mistreating her as an all-around family servant, Catherine humbly pretended to herself that she was in the Holy House of Nazareth and forced herself to look upon her own good mother as the Blessed Virgin! In the end her charity won her parents over, and they allowed her to become a lay sister of the Third Order of St. Dominic, even giving her a private ground-floor room in which she began to mortify herself heroically.

On the evening before her reception into the Order, after undergoing a severe trial in which the devil appeared to her as a handsome young man and offered her a silk gown glittering with jewels, Catherine threw herself before the crucifix and cried out: "My only, my dearest Bridegroom, Thou knowest that I have never desired any but Thee! Come to my aid now, my Saviour!"

Suddenly before Catherine stood the lovely Mother of God, holding a beautiful gold-embroidered robe, and in her soft and gentle voice Mary said: "This garment, my Daughter, I have drawn from the Heart of my Son. It lay hidden in the wound in His side as in a golden casket, and I made it with my own hands." Then in fervent love and humility Catherine bowed her head while Mary clothed her in this heavenly vestment.

During the next four years, in the holy solitude of her little room and in her favorite chapel, the young Saint went through a strict training in self-denial and spiritual development under the personal supervision of Christ and His Mother. Then one Shrove Tuesday after Catherine had prayed all day for perfect faith, Our Lord appeared to her and said:

"Because out of love for Me thou hast renounced all worldly joys and desirest to rejoice in Me alone, I have now resolved solemnly to celebrate My betrothal with thee and to take thee for My bride in the faith."

And as He spoke, there appeared amid many angels His Holy Mother and St. John, St. Paul and St. Dominic. And while the Prophet-King David played sweet music on his harp, Our Lady lovingly took Catherine's hand and placed

ST. CATHERINE OF SIENA (1347-1380) prays with ardent charity for the soul of a criminal about to be executed.

CHRIST AND THE BLESSED VIRGIN personally supervised the strict spiritual development of St. Catherine of Siena, who lived at home, devoting her life entirely to the Crucified Jesus and His Mother. St. Catherine's life was profusely graced by miraculous gifts and mystical experiences. The Saint, a Doctor of the Church, wrote, "Be sure to have recourse to Mary in all things, embracing the holy Cross."

in it that of her Son. Then Jesus put a golden ring on His
bride's finger and said:

"I, thy Creator and Saviour, betroth Myself to thee. I grant
thee a faith that shall never fail...Fear nothing. Thou art
shielded with the armor of faith and thou shalt prevail over
all thy enemies."

Henceforth Catherine was called by God to undertake
an active apostolate, first among the people of Siena, the
City of the Virgin, and then in Pisa and Florence, and eventually in the Papal cities of Avignon and Rome. In fact, more
than any other factor, it was the personal influence, prayers
and sacrifices of this holy young Spouse of Christ, together
with the divine messages and warning which she transmitted, that persuaded the Pope to return to Rome from the
"captivity" in Avignon.

Gradually Catherine drew around her a group of devoted
friends. With others, including two Popes and many prelates and religious, she carried on a rich and inspiring cor-
respondence which now fills six volumes. She would always
begin her letters with these words: "In the name of the Crucified Jesus Christ and of sweet Mary..." and end them
thus: "Sweet Jesus, Jesus Love."

Because Catherine now devoted her life entirely to the
service of the Crucified Jesus and His sweet Mother, Mary
often came to the aid of her saintly young helper. And often
in converting hardened sinners to God, Catherine would
turn with loving confidence to the Mother of Mercy.

Through Mary she obtained the grace of resignation and
peace for an embittered young man who was condemned
to have his head cut off—and she was with him at the end!
"I waited for him at the place of execution," she wrote to
a friend, "and I waited in continual prayer and in the presence of Mary...And before he came, I laid my head on
the block, and I prayed and did violence to Heaven, repeating: 'Mary!' I wanted to obtain the grace that at the last
moment she would give him light and peace..." And Mary
did not disappoint her.

Catherine had long been praying for the right confessor and spiritual director when, one day during Mass in the Dominican Church of Santa Maria Novella in Florence, it seemed to the Saint that Mary herself was standing by her side and indicating a certain Father Raymond of Capua as her appointed guide. Father Raymond became Catherine's spiritual director. And after many years of fruitful collabo-ration with him for the good of souls, Catherine in a letter called this dear friend "my Father and my son whom the sweet Mother Mary gave me."

Twice Catherine received supernatural help from the Blessed Virgin in preparing food for others: once when she was baking bread for her family, and once during a famine after the plague when Catherine obtained five times as much good bread from some poor-quality flour as did a friend working with her—but then, as the Saint wrote to her con-fessor, all the credit was due to Mary and to the Saints and Angels who had helped her.

It was on "the day of Mary," as Catherine called Saturday, that she began to dictate her famous *Dialogue,* an inspired treatise on the Christian virtues. When she founded a small retreat house for her friends, she called it "Our Lady of the Angels."

Twice on special holy days Mary miraculously assisted her young helper. During Mass on New Year's Day Catherine was so overcome with emotion that when she stood up to go to the altar rail for Communion she was about to fall—when the Blessed Virgin with her own gentle but strong hands firmly supported her until she recovered. And one Assumption Day, which was traditionally the greatest feast of the year in the City of the Virgin, Catherine was lying sick in bed, wishing intensely that she might just see the steeple of the Cathedral—and she suddenly found herself in the square before the Cathedral of the Assumption of Our Lady, and she was able to walk right in and attend the solemn High Mass with all her fellow citizens!

Catherine had a touching devotion toward the lovable Babe

of Bethlehem. One Christmas night when she was praying
with her Third Order Sisters in the Church of St. Dominic,
she was given a deeply moving vision of Mary kneeling in
fervent prayer and adoration before the newly born Divine
Child in His radiant crib. Catherine was so profoundly stirred
that she humbly begged the sweet Mother of God to let
her hold the Babe for a moment. With an affectionate smile
Mary took up her Son and gave Him to Catherine. Then
the young Saint lovingly caressed Him and cradled Him
in her arms, kissing His silky little head and whispering
into His tiny ear the names of all who were dear to her. . .

She probably remembered this beautiful mystical
experience during her last season of Advent on earth, a
few months before she died in Rome as a willing victim
for Holy Church, for she then wrote to her friend Andrea
di Vanni a Christmas message which sums up all that she
tried to teach and exemplify as a true helper of Mary in
the service of Christ:

"I beseech you, in this sweet season of Advent and at the
holy Feast of the Nativity, to visit the crib where rests the
meek Lamb. There you will find Mary, a stranger and an
exile, in such great poverty that she has not garments in
which to clothe the Son of God, or a fire to warm Him
who is Life itself, but the beasts warmed Him with their
breath. We may well be ashamed of our pride and our lux-
ury when we see God so deeply abased."

CHAPTER ELEVEN

ST. BERNARDINE OF SIENA
(1380-1444)

O N THE FEAST of the Nativity of Our Lady, September 8, 1380, the same year in which St. Catherine of Siena died, was born another great saint in the City of the Virgin who was destined to become one of the most fervent and eloquent apostles of devotion to Mary in all history.

Soon after being baptized, the little Bernardine Albizzeschi was consecrated to the Mother of God by his devout parents, who had persistently prayed to her for the grace of having a son whom they could offer to the Lord. When the child was only three years old he lost his holy mother, and henceforth he was given an excellent Christian education by his aunt Diana and later by an elderly cousin-and-guardian Tobia, who were both model Catholic women.

With their help, young Bernardine soon learned to love and pray to his sweet Mother in Heaven, and while still a boy he began to fast every Saturday in her honor. As a direct result of his ever-growing devotion to Mary, he became known and respected among his friends for his perfect purity.

77

Whenever he approached a group engaged in talk of a ques-
tionable nature, the boys instinctively warned one another
with a guilty whisper, "Shut up! Here comes Bernardine!"
When he was in his late teens, he joined the Confraternity
of Our Lady of the Angels and took to reciting the Little
Office of the Blessed Virgin every day.

Yet Bernardine was also a very lively and popular youth,
as well as a very handsome one. One day, the eighteen-year-
old Bernardine shocked his guardian, Tobia, by announc-
ing that he was in love with a lovely young lady of Siena!
At first Tobia thought he was joking, as he so often did.
But he insisted very earnestly that he wanted his guardian's
permission to visit the girl every day. "Dear Tobia," he
exclaimed, "my lady friend is so beautiful that I've fallen
head over heels in love with her! She lives just outside the
Camollia Gate. And I have to see her at least once a day—
otherwise I can't sleep at night."

Tobia concealed her fears and disappointment, although
she could hardly believe that all her careful training had
been wasted on Bernardine, who had recently been leading
an increasingly ascetical life. However, she was so disturbed
that she decided to find out who the girl was.

The very next day, therefore, she went to the Camollia
Gate and waited behind some bushes. Soon she saw Bernardine run up eagerly. Disregarding the passersby, he knelt
down, bowed his head a moment, then looked up, blew kisses
and gazed in rapture—at the arch of the city gate, where
there was a beautiful painting of Our Lady surrounded by
angels, in all the glory of her Assumption! Later, after a
reverent bow toward his "lady love," Bernardine modestly
got up and went home, singing gaily. . .

With keen relief and joy, Tobia also went home, and without telling Bernardine that she knew his secret she persuaded
him to reveal it to her, which he did in the following words:

"Since you ask me to do so, my foster mother, I will tell
you something I would not disclose to anyone: I have fallen
in love with the Blessed Virgin Mary, the Mother of God,

to whom I have been devoted since my childhood and in whom I have placed all my hopes. It is she whom I love so intensely, whom I seek, and whom I yearn to see. But since it is not possible as long as I live as an exile in this world to contemplate her in all her loveliness with my own eyes, I decided, out of love for her, to visit the picture of her at the Camollia Gate every day...It makes me happy to kneel before her every day and recommend myself to her intercession, with the certainty of obtaining in the end through her mediation the grace and mercy that I desire. Yes, my 'lady love' and my hope is the Virgin Mother of God!"

Two years later, when thousands of Sienese were dying unattended in agony from the dread Plague, after the help-less director of the Hospital of Our Lady had prayed to her for help — over 500 of his volunteer assistants had already died — Bernardine with twelve companions fearlessly took charge of the institution, and for four terrible months the young Saint tenderly nursed and served and consoled the poor suffering victims of the loathsome pest, heroically dis-regarding his own health and safety! Whenever one of his diseased patients was close to death, Bernardine comforted the dying man or woman by reciting with him or her the following prayer which he had composed himself:

"Holy Mary, Virgin of Virgins, Mother and Daughter of the King of all Kings...safe refuge of sinners, look with compassion on me in this perilous moment. Receive me with mercy when I breathe my last breath. And give me your peace-giving Son. Mary, Mother of Grace, Mother of Mercy, defend us from the enemy, and receive us in the hour of our death. Amen."

When Bernardine was twenty-one, the Blessed Virgin inspired her future messenger to give up everything for the love of God in order to live the simple joy-filled life of a poor and humble son of St. Francis of Assisi. On Septem-ber 8, 1402, again on Mary's birthday and his own, he was received into the Franciscan Order — or, as he said later: "On that same day I was reborn, since...I put on my friar's habit."

And exactly one year later "I promised poverty, chastity, and obedience." And finally, on the same feast of Mary in 1404, young Bernardine was ordained a priest and preached his first sermon — on the Blessed Virgin, of course!

After several years of intensive training in Franciscan spirituality and personal sanctity, Friar Bernardine longed to go forth, like St. Francis, and preach to the multitudes as a fervent messenger of Christ and Mary. But he suffered from what seemed to be a chronic speech defect that prevented him from pronouncing clearly. In this painful predicament he confidently turned to the merciful Mother of God for help. He prayed very fervently, and he asked his brothers in religion to pray that she might free him from this tragic handicap, if it were the will of God that he should devote his life to preaching. And one day while he was thus praying to his dear "lady love" Mary, he saw a mysterious globe of fire come down from Heaven toward him and stop right next to his throat — and he found him-self immediately and completely healed! Henceforth he became famous for his distinct and exquisite enunciation, as well as for his strong and untiring voice. For after this miraculous consecration, which he gratefully attributed to the Blessed Virgin herself, he set forth on his inspired preach-ing apostolate as a true and fervent messenger of Mary call-ing all men back to Christ through her intercession.

During most of the following thirty years St. Bernardine of Siena traveled on foot from one town or village to the next throughout nearly all of northern and central Italy, visiting many cities more than once. Because of his striking personal holiness and purity, and because of his uplifting and inspiring sermons, he was soon celebrated and welcomed everywhere as the greatest popular preacher of his times.

Wherever he went in the increasingly decadent society of early Renaissance Italy, St. Bernardine brought thousands of lax Catholics back to a sincere Christian life. In this vast reform movement, which all historians agree had a profound effect, the humble Friar's principal weapon against evil was the Holy Name of Jesus, which he taught the people to revere and love in the picturesque gold-colored monograms with the letters IHS that he always displayed from the pulpit and distributed among his listeners. With this famous monogram and an appeal for the intercession of his beloved and merciful Mother in Heaven, he also healed many of the sick and even some victims of leprosy.

But all who knew the Saint emphasized that it was in praising Mary that he really surpassed himself in inspired eloquence. In the words of a modern scholar, "Where St. Bernardine truly pours forth all the abundance of his devotion, where his soul completely reveals itself in all its faith, kindness, gentleness and lyricism, and where it truly soars to an angelic height of imaginative vision, is in his sermons dedicated to Our Lady." In the numerous Latin and Italian sermons of the Saint that we have—and many of the latter were taken down word for word by an enthusiastic listener with skill in writing rapidly on wax tablets—there is at least one splendid sermon for each of the feasts of Mary. Another great Franciscan saint who knew Bernardine well testified that "When he spoke to the people on the feasts of Mary about the virtues of the Glorious Virgin, he became so inflamed with fervor that his face seemed to shine and send forth rays of light, like that of a seraph."

We shall quote only the following two brief examples of St. Bernardine's inspired and ardent eloquence in praising Mary:

"O Lady blessed by all and above all things, you are the honor and the preservation of the human race! You are rich in merits and power above every other creature. You are the Mother of God. You are the Mistress of the Universe and the Queen of the World. You are our advocate and the dispenser of all grace...You are a model to which the good look, the consolation of your devoted people, and the beginning of our salvation...Yes, we confess that our tongue is too weak to sing your praises and your greatness. But you, O most sweet Mother, in your kindness have mercy

MADONNA OF THE TEARS, a miraculous portrait of Our Lady and the Infant Jesus located in Trevi, Italy, which shed tears of blood in 1485 in sympathy for plague victims.

ST. BERNARDINE OF SIENA (1380-1444), a Franciscan friar, was miraculously cured of a speech defect by his dear "Lady Love," the Blessed Virgin Mary. He put his newfound eloquence to tremendous use as a true and fervent messenger of Mary, calling all men back to Christ through her intercession.

on our littleness and grant us the grace of being able to praise you more worthily in Paradise forever and ever! Amen."

Then, speaking to his listeners in his familiar way, St. Bernardine would say in the middle of a sermon on the Blessed Virgin: "When you pray the Hail Mary alone without other prayers, with whom do you think you are speaking?...You must know that when you 'hail' Mary, she immediately greets you! Don't think that she is one of those rude women of whom there are so many—on the contrary, she is utterly courteous and pleasant. If you greet her, she will answer you right away and converse with you..."

At least twice during Bernardine's many trips up and down Italy as Mary's tireless messenger, the Blessed Virgin favored her loving servant with a direct personal blessing. After preaching an especially enthusiastic sermon on her Assumption at her lovely little Shrine of Our Lady of the Angels near Assisi, St. Bernardine crossed the valley to the city of Perugia, which was then torn with factional hatreds and steeped in vice, and there he began a historic series of sermons that converted thousands and changed for the better the whole moral life of the community. On the very first day many people saw in the sky the Sorrowful Mother of God weeping with her Divine Son!

And the Saint announced that on one of the following days he would show his listeners the devil! As a result of these sensational developments, nearly everyone in town gathered to hear the holy preacher, and a few days later Bernardine suddenly declared: "Today I am going to keep my word, and I am going to show you not just one but a whole lot of devils!" And then he cried out to the frightened crowd: "Look at one another—and you will see devils all right! For are you not truly devils since you do the work of Satan?" And the great Franciscan Saint was so serious and so severe that no one dared to laugh—rather, under the spell of his burning love for Jesus and Mary they repented and turned away from sin.

Once in Bergamo, when Bernardine was praying to the

Blessed Virgin that his Franciscan Brothers might have a small friary near the town, Mary appeared to the Saint and pointed out a certain farm as being perfectly suited for the purpose. And three years later her grateful servant came back to Bergamo for the dedication of the new monastery. During the solemn procession of all the friars and people through the city streets, suddenly, amid a bright light, there appeared the Glorious Mother of God bearing the Child Jesus in her arms; and while all fell on their knees before this beautiful vision, many saw a radiant star shining on the forehead of Mary's holy messenger!

This striking evidence of divine favor was fully confirmed by God's Church on earth, which, only six years after his peaceful death in 1444, unhesitatingly added the name of this great apostle, Bernardine of Siena, to the list of its Saints in Heaven.

CHAPTER TWELVE

ST. FRANCES OF ROME
(1384-1440)

DURING THE TRAGIC YEARS of the Great Schism at the end of the fourteenth century, Holy Mother Church gave to the world in Rome, the Mother of Churches, the shining example of a perfect Christian mother who con-secrated her life and her lay apostolate to the Mother of God as an Oblate of Mary. For fifty-two of her fifty-six years this remarkable and beautiful woman, St. Frances of Rome, lived in the world a life of such striking holiness and charita-ble service to others that it is hard to understand why she is not yet known and revered by all Catholics as the ideal Christian wife and lay apostle.

Throughout her eventful career as an upper-class Roman matron and foundress of a community of Roman social-worker nuns, Francesca Ponziani was profoundly devoted to the Mother of God. Even as a small child she learned by heart the Little Office of the Blessed Virgin, and she often talked with Mary, whom she called her "dear Mother."

When a girl of only seven, she began to mortify her body

severely and resolved to become a nun. Consequently this young saint underwent at the age of eleven what was perhaps the greatest trial in her whole life: her parents insisted that she marry. Weeping bitterly, Frances ran to be consoled by her wise old Benedictine Father confessor, but under the inspiration of the Holy Ghost he advised her: "If your parents insist, then it must be the will of God. He wants your heart, Frances, but He also requires that you offer yourself to Him by submitting your will completely to His. Therefore, be His faithful servant, no matter in what circumstances He chooses to place you." And so, as the church bells of Rome were ringing the Angelus, young Frances bravely offered up her own will and in spiritual union with Mary humbly pronounced her "Fiat."

For two years the child-bride was deathly sick, until one night St. Alexis of Rome appeared to her and asked her whether she wanted to live. When Frances replied that she wanted only what God willed, the Saint healed her, saying: "The Lord wishes you to remain in this world to glorify Him."

Henceforth Frances lived the happy and busy life of a loving Christian wife and mother. She had two sons and a daughter, whom she trained in sanctity with rare skill and affection. While still in her teens she began to manage with amazing efficiency all the household affairs of a large Roman patrician mansion. She treated her servants with firm and truly supernatural love, nursing them personally when they were sick. She also found many opportunities to sanctify herself in her relations with her mother-in-law. Her extreme generosity toward the poor rather frightened the men in the family, until they saw with stupefaction that Almighty God miraculously replenished their exhausted supplies of grain and wine.

And yet, despite all this activity, Frances somehow found time for daily Mass, meditation and recitation of the Little Office of the Blessed Virgin—and for increasingly austere mortifications. One day, after she had been interrupted during her Office four times in rapid succession without being able to go beyond a certain verse in her prayerbook, she returned to her upstairs oratory the fourth time to find that verse printed in letters of gold, and later St. Paul informed her that this miracle showed *the capital importance in God's sight of willing obedience in one's everyday duties.* (This message was restated by Our Lady in the apparitions at Fatima in 1917.)

When Frances was twenty-four, stark tragedy struck her happy home. In April, 1408, her husband Lorenzo was found outside the city, dying of a sword wound after a battle in which he had fought as one of the Pope's outstanding defenders. As soon as Frances had made him comfortable in their mansion, she begged him to forgive his enemies, and then she prayed so fervently for him that he gradually recovered.

But soon the anti-papal forces broke into Rome, and since Lorenzo could not be moved, Frances was ordered to surrender her eight-year-old son Battista as a hostage. Instead, she fled with the boy. But on the street they met Frances' confessor, and he solemnly warned her: "On behalf of the Lord I say to you—if you want to save him, take him to the Capitol (the enemy headquarters)!" Heartbroken but obedient, Frances gave up her son and went to pray at the nearby Ara Coeli Shrine of the Sorrowful Mother.

There Mary appeared to Frances in her agony, and looking down on her with touching compassion, the Mother of Mercy said: "I am with you—fear nothing. . ." Meanwhile, an officer lifted the boy onto his horse to take him into captivity in Naples, for the papal army was approaching. But the strong horse would not—or could not—move an inch, no matter how much it was whipped or spurred! And after the same unexplainable marvel had happened with three other horses, an awe-struck commander ordered the boy to be returned to his mother.

Nevertheless, having thus learned to trust the Blessed Virgin unconditionally, a few years later Frances was obliged to let her son be captured as a hostage when the enemy troops sacked her home while searching for her husband, who had just been able to escape. Then came the dread Plague, and within a year Frances' other son and baby girl were dead. Yet the grief-stricken mother labored heroically among the sick and the starving, nursing them and bringing them food and clothing in the slums, besides taking many of them into her own devastated mansion. She made herself a sack-like robe from some plain old material and went begging among her rich friends for things which she stuffed into the ample folds of this strange dress. Under her saintly care, miraculous cures became more and more frequent, though she humbly attributed them to God's power and to a medically useless salve.

It was during this harrowing crisis, when she herself had contracted the horrible disease and lay abandoned by all but her beloved sister-in-law, that St. Frances was given an unforgettable series of Dante-esque visions of the various torments of Hell and Purgatory, which later she could never mention without weeping. At this time too—and throughout her life—Frances underwent frequent painful physical persecution by devils. But God also gave her a resplendent archangel who was henceforth her constant guide.

The following year brought peace and the return of her husband and son to their ruined home and destroyed suburban estates. Now Frances had to nurse Lorenzo and teach him again to forgive his enemies. And soon Battista married a very worldly girl with a cruel temper, who for ten years criticized and ridiculed her saintly mother-in-law—until she was finally converted by a stroke of intense physical suffering and by Frances' prayers and merciful kindness. And at last Lorenzo came to realize the rare beauty of the practice of perfect chastity in Christian marriage, as the couple undertook to live a life of continence.

More and more during these years Frances undertook a discreet but very effective apostolate among her many upper-class friends and relatives. By her contagious example and her sincere urging, she inspired a growing number

MARY, "THE SALVATION OF THE ROMAN PEOPLE." The painting shown here, said to have been brought to Rome by St. Helena, was chosen by Pope Liberius to adorn the sanctuary of the Church of St. Mary Major.

ST. FRANCES OF ROME (1384-1440) — wife, mother and widow — in this fresco is portrayed performing a miracle. The Queen of Heaven often invited St. Frances to share feastday ceremonies with the Blessed in Heaven.

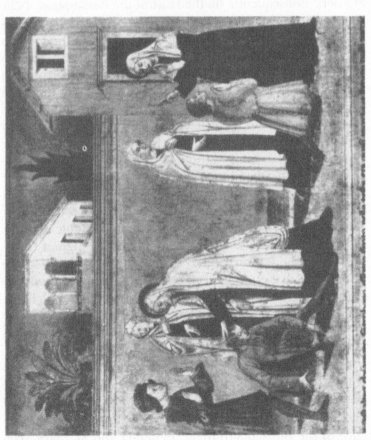

of fashionable ladies to dress and act more modestly, and she often succeeded in completely reconciling various feud-ing noblemen who had been filled with bitter hatred and a lust for vengeance. Her evident sanctity also had a regener-ating influence on several priests and prelates. And now in each successive crisis of the Papacy, she offered herself to God as a willing victim for His Church.

Meanwhile, Frances had enlisted in her extensive charity work a group of fervent lay apostles, and one day she said to these ladies: "I think that we would do something very pleasing to God if we all consecrated ourselves to His Mother!" Consequently, on the Feast of the Assumption, 1425, Frances and seven of her closest friends were accepted as Oblates by the Olivetan Benedictine Fathers in the Church of Santa Maria Nuova.

Two years later, during a pilgrimage to Mary's Portiuncula Shrine near Assisi, after St. Francis himself had appeared to and conversed with the Saint and her two companions on the road, a heavenly voice informed her that the Blessed Virgin wished these lay women to cooperate in founding a new religious congregation.

Thus began what has developed into one of the most remarkable and lasting of Mary's merciful interventions in the history of the Church. It soon became evident that Almighty God wanted a new community of noble servants or Oblates of Mary to give an example of the highest Chris-tian life in the war-torn and dissolute society of Renaissance Rome. Due to Frances' special devotion to the Blessed Vir-gin, "The name of Mary was the pivot around which the whole apostolate of the Oblates revolved." And from now on, the Saint frequently saw the Mother of God in vision "more clearly than her Oblates saw one another."

During the eight years of gradual preparation which passed before the Oblates took up residence in a house of their own, Frances often dictated to her confessor the words of their Rule which were given to her by St. Paul, in the pres-ence of the Blessed Virgin, St. Benedict and St. Mary Mag-

dalen, who were the heavenly patrons of the new community. Thus four Lents each year were prescribed, as well as
many minute details of daily life. Without being cloistered,
these young and middle-aged arisocratic ladies were to devote
their time to prayer and charity work among the poor.

Now Mary often invited Frances to attend various feastday ceremonies with the Blessed in Heaven, and during the
beautiful celebrations in honor of the great Queen of Heaven
the Saint contemplated Mary in all the Mysteries of her
glorious life. She often described to her friends the Virgin's
three lovely crowns, symbolizing her humility, her virginity
and her glory.

But it was at Christmas that Frances enjoyed the most
thrilling mystical experiences. One year while she was holding the Babe of Bethlehem in her arms, softly humming
a lullaby, Mary playfully tried to take Him away from her,
and then Jesus Himself, after urging Frances to be generous
in sacrifices, escaped from her hands. Another Christmas,
when Mary appeared to her with the Christ Child on her
knees and the Saint begged to be allowed to caress Him,
His Mother smiled and said: "But you will not be able to
hold Him up—He is so heavy!" And with her quick Italian
wit Frances replied: "O Queen of Heaven, don't worry—He
will be able to hold Himself up all right!" At Christmas,
1432, Frances spent forty-eight hours in blissful ecstasy.

Henceforth, as Frances said, "I no longer belong to myself.
I am an Oblate consecrated to the great Queen of the Angels.
It is she who is my teacher and my patroness. As for me,
I am her servant, her subject, her slave!" And later, after
she had seen Mary and the Saints praying for Rome when
it was threatened with war and intrigue, Frances explained
thus to her Oblates what this consecration involves:

"My daughters, the Virgin asks us for tears, prayers,
penances. It is up to you to supply what others fail to do—
that is your vocation: to pray and to do penance for yourselves and for others. You are victims destined to appease
the wrath of God...The Virgin will truly call you her Oblates

when she sees you offer up your bodies and your souls as a sacrifice to the Lord through your prayers and mortifica· tions. You are few, but be sure that if you are fervent and persevere, you will obtain help, and you will end a great evil. Yes, soon you will see the fruit of your tears. . ."

In 1436, a few months after her husband's death, the Saint at last joined her beloved Oblates in their convent. But she who had longed to spend her whole life as a cloistered nun was destined to enjoy the religious life for only four years, during which she served her Sisters as a firm yet loving and humble Mother Superior. And on March 9, 1440, when Our Lady's Oblate and model lay apostle left this world for Heaven, her last act on earth was to finish reading her Little Office of the Blessed Virgin Mary.

ST. FRANCES OF ROME

CHAPTER THIRTEEN

ST. NICHOLAS OF FLÜE
(1417-1487)

O<small>N</small> MAY 15, 1947, the Feast of the Ascension, His Holiness Pope Pius XII solemnly canonized one of the most extraordinary saints in the history of the Church: St. Nicholas of Flüe, known as "Brother Klaus," who was in turn a prominent civic leader, soldier, patriot, father of a large family—and then for nearly twenty years a holy hermit who took no other nourishment than Holy Communion and whose pacifying influence was so decisive in the turbulent history of his country that for over four hundred and fifty years he has been considered the Patron Saint of Switzerland. And today the sturdy and sober inhabitants of that healthy little Christian democracy believe that it was largely due to his intercession that they were not drawn into our two World Wars.

In the year 1467, Nikolaus von der Flüe was a highly respected and prosperous landowner who lived with his family of five boys and four girls on an estate in a fertile valley about twenty miles south of the picturesque Swiss

city of Lucerne. At the age of fifty he could look back on
a full and rich life, in the course of which he had served
his neighbors and his country as a soldier and as a local
judge and official. He had built his own substantial home
and raised a happy and devout family with his beautiful
wife, Dorothy.

But for the last two years Nicholas had been deeply troubled. Ever since his childhood he had felt drawn to a life
of self-denial and prayer. As a boy he had loved to go off
into the fields alone and meditate whenever he could. Then
too, the cruelties of war and the injustices of public affairs
had made him turn more and more to God. Yet he always
knew that he was not meant to be a priest or a monk. So
he had become a model husband and father. He and his
wife liked to pray together at wayside shrines of Our Lady.
At work in the fields with his sons, he often sang hymns.
And each evening the whole family gathered to pray the
family Rosary, after which Nicholas gave them all his loving
blessing. But every night he got up and spent hours in prayer.
He had composed for himself the following short but powerful formula, which summed up all the deepest desires of
his strong Christian heart:

"My Lord and my God, take from me all that keeps me
from You.

"My Lord and my God, give me all that brings me closer
to You.

"My Lord and my God, take me from myself and give
me to Yourself."

And God answered his prayer.

One day when Nicholas was working around his home,
three very distinguished Strangers appeared to him, and
the First among Them said: "Nicholas, do you want to give
yourself wholly to Us?"

He replied: "I give myself to no one but Almighty God,
whom I want to serve with all my heart and soul!"

The three Strangers were so pleased that They laughed
joyfully, and Their Leader said to Nicholas: "If you have

offered yourself to serve God forever, I make you this solemn promise: when you reach your seventieth year, the Merciful Lord will have pity on your labors and will deliver you from all your burdens. Therefore I urge you to persevere faithfully until then. And I will give you the banner of the victorious army in life eternal...I leave you a cross to carry, in remembrance of Us."

Nicholas realized that the Blessed Trinity was calling him to devote the next twenty years of his life completely to the service of God.

"While I was in that state," he said later, "the priest who was my friend and confidant came to see me...and I told him what was troubling me...then he taught me how to meditate on the incidents of Our Lord's Sorrowful Passion at the seven liturgical hours...and so I often went to a solitary retreat near my house in order to meditate on the Passion. And thus I spent two years..."

Finally, however, as a result of several other visions, Nicholas became convinced that God was calling him to give up everything, to leave his beloved family, his home, and his country, in order to live abroad as a hermit. With keen anguish of soul he talked the matter over with his devoted wife, for this extraordinary vocation meant a real personal sacrifice for them both, even though materially the entire family would have perfect security, since the oldest sons were now fully able to support their mother and the other children. Dorothy and Nicholas prayed fervently together to Mary for guidance. And at last, after a heroic struggle with herself, Dorothy sadly resigned herself to what they both knew to be undeniably the will of God. And on October 16, 1467, sorrowfully yet with a new peace in his heart, Nicholas said farewell to his weeping wife and dear children, gave them all his last blessing and set out as a penniless pilgrim, barefoot and bareheaded, in a long gray-brown robe, taking with him nothing but a staff and a rosary.

He went toward Alsace, which at that time was a center of ardent mystics known as the Friends of God. But after he had gone about fifty miles, a vision convinced the future Patron Saint of Switzerland that he should stay among his own people. He therefore returned to his valley, where friends discovered him some days later, praying and fasting in the woods.

Soon the report began to circulate throughout the region that the well-known farmer Nicholas of Flüe had become a hermit and was apparently living in the snow-covered hills entirely without food. Naturally an official investigation was launched. For one month every approach to his retreat was carefully watched—and the sensational rumor became an incredible but irrefutably demonstrated fact. Henceforth Nicholas was called Brother Klaus, and many people already spoke of him as "the living Saint." Within a few years his fame had spread through the Swiss Cantons and most of the German Empire. Even before a Bishop examined and approved his case, Nicholas' proud neighbors built him a tiny hut and chapel where he was divinely guided to make his hermitage, in the lovely green valley of the Ranft, about an hour's walk from his home.

It is deeply significant that Brother Klaus dedicated his little chapel to the Virgin Mother of God, whom an old chronicle calls "his special patroness," and to whom he was intensely devoted all his life. An eye-witness testified after his death that as a young soldier Nicholas went to war "with a sword in one hand and a rosary in the other." All his portraits and statues show him holding in one hand his plain rosary with its large wooden beads. And at a time when the Immaculate Conception of the Mother of God was still a subject for debate among theologians, Brother Klaus did not hesitate to explain to a friend in his quaint and simple way:

"Now I want to speak to you also about the pure servant-girl Mary who is yet a Queen of Heaven and earth and who was foreseen by Divine Wisdom. The same invested her as soon as God decided to create her. So she was conceived in the mind of the All-High Lord before she was conceived in her mother's womb. And the same grace was in that union with great sanctity. That is why she is pure, gentle and immaculate."

In fact, Brother Klaus left his solitary retreat only to honor Mary. Every year he took part in the solemn procession in Lucerne on the Feast of the Annunciation. And he was often seen at the famous Shrine of Our Lady of the Hermits, for Our Lady was especially dear to him under that title. His inner recollection in prayer was so intense on these devout pilgrimages that once, at the end of the fifty-mile trip over the hills, he had only just finished the single Our Father which he had begun to pray on leaving the Ranft.

No doubt the Merciful Mother of God often rewarded Brother Klaus with extraordinary graces, and in fact today another lovely little chapel stands on a spot not far from his hut where Mary appeared to him and conversed with him. And surely it was the Queen of Peace who inspired him to urge the many pilgrims who visited him to love and practice peace.

The saintly hermit revealed to a few intimate friends several of the mystical visions which had been given him by God. And the Blessed Virgin plays a major role in the most touching and beautiful of those, which we shall narrate in the simple language of the old chronicle:

One night when Brother Klaus was nearing the end of his twenty-years' fast and life as a holy hermit, while still awake he heard a strong, clear Voice call him, saying: "Come to your Father and see what He is doing." Then he seemed to be in a great hall in a fine castle with a few persons dressed in white robes. And the One who had called him said: "Here is he who comforted Your Son and came to His help in His suffering and need. Be grateful to him and thank him."

Then through the palace came a great and wonderful Person dressed in a white robe like a priest at Mass. And He placed both arms on Brother Klaus' shoulders and drew him to Himself and thanked him with fervent love in His

Foto Reinhard, Sachseln

THE HERMITAGE CELL of St. Nicholas of Flüe.

ST. NICHOLAS OF FLÜE, beloved Swiss saint (1417-1487), led an unusually varied life. He was a husband and the father of nine children, a civic leader, soldier, and, finally, a hermit. The Saint received a visit from the Blessed Trinity, and after several additional visions he bid his family farewell and left his earthly possessions behind. Henceforth called "Brother Klaus," the Saint spent the final twenty years of his life as a holy hermit, often interrupted by his countrymen, who called upon him to settle political disputes.

heart for having so well helped His Son in His need. And He went away.

Then there came through the palace a very beautiful great Lady, also dressed in spotless white. And she too placed her hands on Brother Klaus' shoulders and pressed him to her heart with tender love and thanked him. And then she left.

Now near him Brother Klaus saw the Son seated on a throne and clad in a similar robe, except that it was spattered with red spots like blood. And the Son bowed toward him and thanked him gratefully for having helped Him in His suffering. And Brother Klaus looked down and saw that he, too, was wearing a white robe with red spots, like the Son...

Thus did the Eternal Father, the pure Mother of God and her Divine Son reward Brother Klaus, "the Living Saint," for giving the world such a noble example of Christian self-denial, holy living and complete dedication to the service of the King of Kings. But perhaps most of all they thanked him for having taught his Swiss brothers in Christ to love peace and to live in the peace of God.

For this very typical Swiss was profoundly revered and honored by his fellow countrymen during his lifetime. As one old account says, "This Brother Klaus exercised great authority among the Swiss. In all their doubts and difficulties they turned to him at all times, and they looked upon his advice and exhortations as an inspired oracle..." In fact, on more than one historical occasion he played a decisive pacifying role in major political crises. For centuries every Swiss child has been taught that at the crucial Diet of Stans, on December 22, 1481, when the delegates of the several Allied Cantons were about to separate in bitter disagreement, the only factor that saved the Swiss Federation from disintegration and civil war was an impressive and inspired secret message from Brother Klaus which a priest brought at the last moment—"and within an hour a unanimous settlement was reached," such was the hermit's prestige.

On his seventieth birthday, March 21, 1487, as the Three Strangers had promised, the Good Lord had pity on Brother Klaus' labors for Him and rewarded the grand old hermit with the banner of victory in life everlasting.

And then began that period of 460 years during which his cause for beatification and canonization advanced slowly but surely, despite one delay after another, with the enthusiastic support of three great Saints: St. Charles Borromeo, St. Peter Canisius and St. Robert Bellarmine. However, after the Beatification in 1669, it would seem that Almighty God wanted His Holy Church to withhold the final hour of the Canonization until the Armageddons of this century, in order that in the hour of its great need humanity might learn from the worthy patron of the oldest Christian democracy in the world how to practice simplicity and piety and how to live in peace and charity toward all men. Indeed, a recent article entitled "A Patron for Peace Planners" aptly declares that "we need a saint to enter the conference halls and remind men again in the words of Brother Klaus: 'PEACE IS ALWAYS IN GOD!'"

The most striking proof of Brother Klaus' effectiveness in the cause of peace is the fact that today most Swiss men, women and children are humbly and gratefully thanking their beloved patron for having kept them out of the two terrible World Wars of our times. In 1917, when the German and French armies threatened to overflow into Switzerland and when the Swiss people themselves were sharply divided by partiality toward one or the other of the two combatants, the timely celebration of the 500th anniversary of Brother Klaus' birth served to unite the whole nation, and thus Nicholas again inspired his fellow countrymen to remain faithful to his message of peace and union. And in May, 1940, when Hitler's Panzer Divisions were swirling around the frontiers of Switzerland and every Swiss bravely faced the prospect of invasion and war at any moment, one night near the spot where Brother Klaus had been led to return to his own people, several hundred persons saw in the sky a great protecting hand extended over their free territory. After an official investigation had definitely established that this significant phenomenon could not have had a natural cause, the devout Swiss were sure that their patron was protecting his country.

In recent years, two former Presidents of Switzerland have expressed the deepest convictions of their fellow citizens in these words: "Nicholas of Flüe is alive today among us and above us. Today we all feel his presence and the influence of his spirit" (Philip Etter). "Brother Klaus is the strongest moral factor in Switzerland today" (Giuseppe Motta).

And now at last, with the Vicar of Christ officially proclaiming the simple, humble and selfless patriot-mystic *Saint* Nicholas of Flüe, all the world may learn the profound truth of the comment which St. Charles Borromeo made when, after praying for two hours at Brother Klaus' hermitage on August 22, 1570, he rose to his feet and declared with impressive gravity: *"He was indeed a great saint!"*

CHAPTER FOURTEEN

ST. IGNATIUS OF LOYOLA
(1491-1556)

W HEN, DURING THE fifteenth century, the leaders of the
Protestant revolt began to "reform" God's revealed religion, Divine Providence chose one man to save and rebuild
the Church of Christ: a young Spanish nobleman named
Inigo de Loyola. And as we shall see in significant excerpts
from his autobiography, this extraordinary man who became
the founder and commander-in-chief of the vast army of
well-trained soldiers of God known as the Society of Jesus
was converted in only one year by the Blessed Virgin herself, from a very worldly life to one of heroic sanctity.

A few months before he died, St. Ignatius dictated to a
friend, in the third person, an account of his youth and
conversion, in which he admitted that "up to his twenty-
sixth year, his heart was fascinated by the vanities of the
world. His special delight was in the military life, and he
seemed to be led by a strong and empty desire of making
a great name for himself."

As a youth Ignatius was proud and ambitious, a great

reader of tales of chivalry, and quite a lady's man. While attached to the service of a nobleman, he always bore arms and wore an open cloak. He was very fastidious about his appearance, took much care of his delicate hands and long hair, and dressed in bright colors.

He once fell in love with a beautiful lady of the highest nobility and used to spend "three and four hours at a time picturing to himself how he would travel to the city where she was, how he would speak to her, what brilliant and charming expressions he would use, and what warlike exploits he would perform to please her."

At this time, according to one of his closest friends, "he did not live in harmony with his religion and did not keep himself from sin. He was particularly inclined to gambling, affairs with women, and duels." Once Ignatius and one of his brothers were arrested for some unspecified escapade, perpetrated at night, which had caused considerable damage. That he was a typically hot-blooded Spaniard is proved by the fact that one day when some men on a street happened to crowd him to the wall, Ignatius drew his sword and pursued them—"and if he had not been held back, it would have ended in a murder," according to an eye-witness.

He was also a loyal patriot and a fearless soldier. When the French invaded his country, during Mary's month in the year 1521, Ignatius confessed his sins to a fellow soldier in a chapel of Our Lady and bravely fought off a six-hours' siege, until a cannonball struck his legs, breaking one and wounding the other. Soon after he fell, his troops surrendered.

Despite his extremely painful wounds, he was carried to the Loyola family home on a stretcher. The doctors then decided to break his leg again in order to reset it correctly. During this "butchery," as Ignatius called it, he stoically gave no sign of suffering, except for tightly clenching his fists. But soon he lost strength and could not eat. On the Feast of St. John the Baptist the doctors gave up hope for his recovery and advised him to make his last Confession. And on the Feast of Sts. Peter and Paul he received the Last Sacraments, for the doctors expected him to die that night.

But Christ the King had other plans for His future soldier. As Ignatius put it, "He was already devoted to St. Peter" (the Patron Saint of the Loyola family), "and therefore it pleased Our Lord that *that* very night he began to get better, and within a few days he was considered out of danger." But the worldly young Spaniard was not yet converted, for when he saw that one leg was deformed and shorter than the other, "out of vanity, because he still wanted to spend his life at court," he willingly underwent a still more painful operation which involved the sawing off of a protruding bone, after which he had to stay in bed for many weeks while the wound healed.

To pass the long hours, Ignatius asked for some of the romances and novels which he liked so much. But by God's design it happened that the only reading material available was a life of Christ and a book on the lives of the Saints. Now the future Saint himself will tell us the striking story of his conversion:

"By frequently reading these books he began to acquire some love for spiritual things. This reading led his mind to meditate on holy subjects, yet sometimes it wandered to thoughts which he had been accustomed to dwell on before. While going through the life of Our Lord and the Saints, he began to reflect and say to himself: 'What if I should do what St. Francis did? What if I should act like St. Dominic? St. Francis did this—therefore I will do it too!' These heroic resolutions remained for a time, and then other vain and worldly thoughts followed. But in these thoughts there was this difference: when he thought of worldly things it gave him great pleasure, but afterwards he found himself dry and sad; but when he thought of journeying to Jerusalem and of living only on herbs and practicing austerities, he found pleasure not only while thinking of them, but also when he had ceased.

"By experience he learned that one train of thought left

him sad, the other joyful. This was his first discovery in spiritual matters. When gradually he recognized the different spirits by which he was moved—one of the Spirit of God, the other the Devil—and when he had gained considerable spiritual enlightenment from reading religious books, he began to think more seriously of his past life and how much penance he should do to expiate his past sins. The holy desire to imitate saintly men came to his mind. His resolve was not more definite than to promise that with the help of divine grace he too would do what they had done. His one wish after his recovery was to make a pilgrimage to Jerusalem. He fasted frequently and scourged himself to satisfy the desire for penance which ruled a soul filled with the spirit of God. The vain thoughts gradually decreased..."

Then, during the glorious Feast of Our Lady's Assumption, there occurred that decisive intervention of Mary which permanently changed the worldly young Spanish soldier into a great and fervent and pure saint of God.

One night, while Ignatius was praying, "he distinctly saw the Blessed Mother of God with the Holy Infant Jesus! And at this sight, for quite some time, he was overwhelmed with consolation. And he remained with such disgust for his whole past life and especially for impurity that it seemed to him as if all the impressions which had hitherto been imprinted on his soul were torn away." From that moment until the end of his life, "he never again gave the least consent to impure sin. Consequently, the experience may be considered as having been from God..."

Henceforth "his brother and all in the house noticed from his appearance what a great change had taken place in his soul. Meanwhile, he continued his reading and kept the holy resolution he had made. At home, his conversation was wholly devoted to divine matters and had a spiritual influence on others." He proceeded to make an intensive study of the Gospels and to write out all their most important passages in a notebook. Thus he reverently filled three hundred pages, using red ink for Christ's words and blue ink for those of Mary. As soon as he could get up, he spent much of his time in the Chapel of the Annunciation in his home. Now he also "began his habit of taking the discipline every night. During these days his greatest source of consolation was to gaze at the heavens and stars at night, which he did frequently and for a long time, experiencing in his soul a very generous impulse to serve Our Lord." And he seriously considered becoming a Carthusian monk after his pilgrimage to the Holy Land.

As soon as his health permitted, he left home, taking with him a picture of the Sorrowful Mother, a prayerbook containing the Little Office of the Blessed Virgin, and his notebook of the Gospels. Setting out on his pilgrimage and at the same time on his new life, Ignatius went immediately to the nearest shrine of Mary and spent the night there in prayer, thanking Our Lady for his conversion, praying for strength for his journey, and receiving such stirring consolations that thirty years later he still spoke of them with intense gratitude.

Traveling on, he collected some money owed to him and spent half of it on the restoration of a picture of the Blessed Virgin in a church on the way. And it was probably at this time that he solemnly made, before God and through the mediation of Mary, a private vow of perpetual chastity.

Yet, as he admitted later, "his knowledge of spiritual things was still very obscure. To do something great for the glory of his God, to imitate saintly men in all they had done before him—this was his only object in his practice of external mortification."

Now Our Lady put her newly enlisted soldier to a remarkable test. A Moslem who rode along with Ignatius for a while insisted, despite all argument, that the Mother of Christ could not have remained a virgin after the birth of her Son. Then the Moslem rode on, leaving Ignatius "sorely troubled and feeling impelled by a strong impulse to hasten after him and kill him. But after much internal conflict he

Heinemann/Schamoni

ST. IGNATIUS LOYOLA (1491-1556), founder of the Society of Jesus, or the Jesuit Order, was a Spanish nobleman who underwent conversion from a worldly life, becoming a great spiritual leader. His awakening came when he read the life of Christ and lives of the Saints, after which the Blessed Mother and Infant Jesus intervened in his life through a remarkable vision.

ST. IGNATIUS read his vows in front of this thirteenth-century mosaic of Our Lady and her divine Son.

remained in doubt and could not decide what to do." Finally he resolved to settle all his doubts in the following novel way: if on coming to the next crossroad his horse followed the Moslem, he would pursue him and kill him. "Through the Providence of God" the horse took the other direction, and Ignatius learned a valuable lesson.

Next he went to the famous old Shrine of Our Lady of Montserrat in order to spend a night in prayer before her altar and thus, like the knights of chivalry, to become one of her soldiers by taking up the arms of Christ. And on the eve of the Feast of the Annunciation, 1522, after a General Confession that lasted three days, the twenty-nine-year-old Ignatius Loyola, dressed only in a piece of sackcloth "filled with prickly wooden fibers...hastened at nightfall to the church, where he threw himself on his knees before the altar of the Blessed Mother of God, and there, now kneeling, now standing, with staff in hand, he passed the entire night. After receiving the Blessed Sacrament, he left the town at daybreak."

Ignatius now went to a small nearby town named Manresa, which was situated in a lovely valley and which had a cathedral and eleven other churches dedicated to the Mother of God. Here the holy knight of Mary begged alms for his living and spent most of his time in the hospital and the churches. He also taught catechism to children and began to speak about religion to all who associated with him. Here too he underwent various spiritual trials and mystical experiences. He went to Confession and Holy Communion once a week, and during Mass every day he read the Passion in one of the Gospels, which filled his soul "with a joyful feeling of uninterrupted calm." He often spent hours meditating in a lonely cave outside the town, which has now become the famous Shrine of Manresa. He lived in a Dominican monastery and "kept up his usual custom of praying on bended knees for seven hours a day, and scourged himself three times a day and during the night."

During this extraordinary novitiate Mary's soldier, no

doubt through her intercession, received numerous heavenly favors. "Once while reciting on the steps of the monastery the Little Hours in honor of the Blessed Virgin, his vision carried him beyond the earth. He seemed to see the Holy Trinity, and this vision affected him so much that he could not keep from weeping and sobbing. During the rest of his life, whenever he prayed to the Holy Trinity, he experienced great devotion."

"Often in prayer, and for a long time, he saw with the eyes of his soul Our Lord and His Humanity. . . perhaps twenty or even forty times. He saw the Blessed Virgin like-wise. These visions gave him such strength that he often thought that even if Holy Scripture did not bear witness to these mysteries of the Faith, still, from what he had seen, it would be his duty to lay down his life for them."

It was during his stay of ten months at Manresa that St. Ignatius wrote the first draft of his famous *Spiritual Exercises,* a series of systematically graded examinations of conscience and meditations on the life of Christ, designed for a thirty-days' retreat, which have in thousands of cases converted retreatants — including many well-known priests and lay apostles — to a new life of loving, selfless service to Christ. While Jesus and Mary may not have literally dictated these powerful Spiritual Exercises to the Saint, it is certain that they did directly or indirectly inspire him to write them.

Such was the thorough ascetical and mystical training which the Blessed Virgin gave to her chosen soldier before sending him out into the world in order, like Francis of Assisi, to rebuild the Church of Christ.

After a pilgrimage to the Holy Land, Ignatius studied for the priesthood in Spain and at Paris, where he gathered around him a small group of outstanding followers like the future St. Francis Xavier. Later in Rome they founded the great Society of Jesus, which for four centuries has gener-ously given to Holy Mother Church hundreds of saintly schol-ars, educators and missionaries.

To Mary's soldier, St. Ignatius Loyola, more than to any

other man belongs the glory of having regenerated and saved the Church of Christ at a time when, like today, it was being attacked by powerful groups of men who were determined to destroy it.

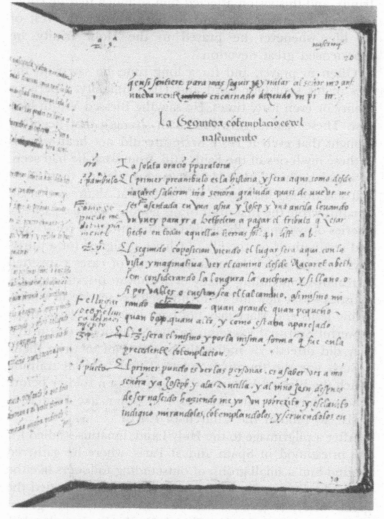

THE SPIRITUAL EXERCISES of St. Ignatius Loyola have been employed by countless retreatants since their first publication in 1548. Pictured here is a page from the Saint's handwritten work.

CHAPTER FIFTEEN

ST. TERESA OF AVILA
(1515-1582)

THE GREAT SPANISH Carmelite reformer, St. Teresa of
Avila, has been rightly called "one of the greatest, most
attractive and widely appreciated women whom the world
has ever known." Her friends exclaimed, "Thanks be to God
that He has let us see a saint whom we can imitate!" With
all her holiness and mystical gifts, Teresa always had a delight-
ful sense of humor.

She was one of those apostolic souls, like Catherine of
Siena, whose devotion to Jesus Christ was so intense and
whose mystical union with Him was so intimate that the
Blessed Virgin might inevitably seem to have played only
a humble minor role her life. Nevertheless, the marvelous
writings of St. Teresa (which we shall quote extensively) reveal
that the merciful Mother of God not only helped the Saint
in her heroic apostolate on numerous important occasions,
but also strikingly rewarded Teresa's fervent devotion in
several of the most significant of her many mystical
experiences.

In her remarkable autobiography, St. Teresa wrote that her mother's care in training her to "pray and be devoted to Our Lady. . . began to wake me up when I was six or seven years old." Every evening after supper, her devout family prayed a family prayer together. With one of her brothers, little Teresa used to enjoy reading the lives of the saints and martyrs — "and I had a great desire to die a martyr's death." The two children even made an unsuccessful attempt to run away and die as martyrs among the Moors. Then they built a hermitage in their garden, in which they prayed the Rosary and played with their friends at being monks and nuns. Young Teresa, whenever she was troubled, loved to walk to a nearby hospital chapel and kneel for a long time before an unusually lifelike and compassionate-looking statue of Our Lady of Charity.

Her mother died when Teresa was about thirteen, and many years later the Saint wrote: "When I began to under-stand my loss, in my affliction I went to an image of Our Lady and with many tears implored her to be my Mother. I did this in my simplicity, and I believe that it helped me, for by experience I have found that the Royal Virgin has helped me whenever I have recommended myself to her. And at last she has brought me back to herself."

During her girlhood Teresa had "wasted hours night and day" reading romantic novels: "So completely was I mastered by this passion that I thought I could never be happy with-out a new book. And this was the beginning of lukewarm-ness in my good desires. I began to pay much attention to how I dressed, and to wish to please others by my appear-ance. I took great care of my hands and my hair, and used perfumes and all vanities within my reach, and they were many." She also began to spend hours in frivolous conversa-tions with girlfriends.

But soon her father sent Teresa to the Augustinian con-vent school of Our Lady of Grace, and gradually, by the grace of God through Mary, though not without considera-ble conflict of soul, Teresa resolved to become, not a saint, but just a good nun. For, like Ignatius of Loyola, she had learned to enjoy reading the lives of the Saints, instead of the novels of which she now wrote, "I understood now the harm they had done me."

When she reached the age of twenty, despite her father's temporary opposition, Teresa secretly left her home and entered the somewhat lax Carmelite Convent of Our Lady of the Incarnation in Avila. And on November 2, 1537, she was professed and "took the habit of the Glorious Virgin of Mount Carmel."

The following summer, after months of sickness and solitary prayer, just before the Feast of the Assumption, the young nun apparently died; her grave was dug, but as her funeral was about to begin, she opened her eyes and said to her mourning and praying relatives: "Why have you called me back?" She had just had an unforgettable first mystical experience, during which she was shown in vision the horrors of Hell and her own future destiny: she saw communities of nuns being organized by her efforts, many souls entering Heaven, and finally her own death.

For the next three years Teresa was partly paralyzed and suffered intensely, until she took St. Joseph as her special patron and he miraculously healed her. All the rest of her life she was so devoted to him that she could write: "I cannot recall that I have ever asked him at any time for anything which he has not granted." And it is largely due to her example and influence that popular devotion to St. Joseph has increased so marvelously in modern times.

Although Teresa still took too much pleasure in worldly visits and conversations, she now began to advance in mental prayer, and soon she was given various supernatural favors, as God drew the future Saint more and more to Himself. Our Lord appeared to her and conversed with her frequently, as He continued to do all the rest of her life. But for a long time her friends and confessors were afraid that she was being deceived by the devil, and she had to endure much anguish and misunderstanding. Turning to Mary for consolation, Teresa made a long and difficult pilgrimage over the mountains to the famous Spanish Shrine of Our Lady of Guadalupe.

Finally, after nearly twenty years of inner suffering and purification through mortification and prayer, she was freed from this trial when the great Franciscan mystic and reformer, St. Peter of Alcantara, visited her and declared that she was certainly inspired by God. She first confessed to this holy man in the Church of Our Lady of the Annunciation, and she gratefully thanked Mary for his valuable assistance.

It was at this period in her life, as Teresa wrote that, "one day—it was the Feast of the Assumption of Our Lady, the Queen of the Angels—Our Lord was pleased to grant me this grace: In a trance He made me behold her going up to Heaven, the joy and solemnity of her reception there, as well as the place where she is now. To describe it is more than I can do. The joy that filled my soul at the sight of such great glory was excessive. The effects of the vision were great: it made me long to endure still greater trials, and I had an intense desire to serve Our Lady, because of her great merits."

Henceforth so many important events in Teresa's life occurred on feasts of Mary that she once wrote: "Today is the vigil of Our Lady of August. Our joys and sorrows come to us on her feasts, as though from her."

And on the Feast of the Assumption in 1561, when the forty-six-year-old Saint was planning to counteract the Protestant war against Christ's Church by founding a small community of holy contemplative nuns under the strict primitive Carmelite Rule, Teresa underwent a decisive supernatural experience which marked the turning point in her life between an intensive self-sanctification and an incredibly active exterior apostolate.

"I was in the church of the monastery of the Order of the glorious St. Dominic, thinking of the events of my wretched life and of the many sins which in times past I had confessed in that church. I fell into so profound a trance that I was beside myself, as it were. I sat down, and it seemed as if I could neither see the Elevation nor hear Mass. I thought then that I saw myself clothed with a garment of excessive whiteness and splendor. At first I did not see who was putting it on me. Afterwards I saw Our Lady on my right and my father St. Joseph on my left, clothing me with that garment. I was given to understand that I was then cleansed from my sins. When I had thus been clad—I was filled with the utmost delight and joy—Our Lady seemed at once to take me by both hands. She said that I pleased her very much by being devout to the glorious St. Joseph, that I might rely on it that my desires about the convent would be accomplished, that I was to be afraid of no failure whatever, because they would watch over us and because her Son had promised to be with us—and as proof of this, she was going to give me this jewel. Then she seemed to throw around my neck a most splendid necklace of gold, from which hung a cross of much value...The beauty which I saw in Our Lady was exceedingly great, although I could not make out anything particular in form or features, but it was rather the whole shaping of her face, clothed in white with the utmost splendor, which was not dazzling but soft. I did not see St. Joseph so clearly...Our Lady seemed to be quite young. When they had been with me thus for a while—I too was in the greatest bliss and joy, greater than I had ever had before, and I wished never to part with it—I thought I saw them go up to Heaven with a multitude of angels. I was left in great loneliness, though so comforted and uplifted, so recollected and stirred that for some time I was not able to move or speak. I was now possessed of a strong desire to be consumed for the love of God. I could never have a doubt that the vision came from God. It left me in the greatest consolation and peace."

"At another time I saw Our Lady putting a cope of exceeding whiteness" on a certain holy Dominican Father. "She told me that she gave him that cope in consideration of the service he had rendered her by helping to found this house, that it was a sign that she would preserve his soul pure for the future and that he should not fall into mortal sin."

At last St. Teresa was ready to begin her dramatic twenty-year campaign for the reform of the Carmelite Order. During this period, despite bitter opposition and cruel persecution and tremendous practical difficulties, Mary's apostolic reformer founded seventeen small communities of fervent contemplative nuns—eleven of which were dedicated to St. Joseph, and four to Mary—and she inspired the holy young priest, St. John of the Cross, to do likewise with the Carmelite Friars. Teresa once expressed the basic philosophy of her reform in these words: *"When I see the great necessities of the Church, I am so afflicted by them that it seems to me mockery to be troubled by anything else...for I see that one person wholly perfect, with true fervor of love for God, will be worth more than many who are lukewarm."* And at the very beginning of her apostolate, "One day after Communion Our Lord commanded me to labor with all my might for this end. He made me great promises—that the convent would certainly be built, that He would take great delight therein, that St. Joseph would keep guard at one door and Our Lady at the other, that Christ would be in the midst of us."

After her first foundation, in Avila, of a poor little reformed convent without any endowment, "While praying in the chapel, I saw Christ, who welcomed me with great affection, placed a crown on my head and thanked me for what I had done for His Mother."

"On another occasion, when all of us remained praying in the choir after Compline, I saw Our Lady in exceeding great glory in a white mantle with which she seemed to cover us all. I understood by that the high degree of glory to which Our Lord would raise the religious of this house."

And the humble Saint gratefully advised her nuns: "Praise Him, my Daughters, that you may truly be the daughters of that Lady, and thus you need not be ashamed that I am a wicked person, since you have such a good Mother. Imitate her, and reflect that the greatness of this Lady and the good of having her as a Patron have been such that my sins and my being what I am have not been enough to ruin this holy Order...My Daughters, let us in some measure imitate the great humility of the most holy Virgin, whose habit we wear, though we should feel confused in calling ourselves her nuns. However much we seem to humble our-selves, we fall far short of being worthy daughters of such a Mother..."

As proof of her intense devotion and gratitude to Mary, Teresa not only placed a statuette of Our Lady over one of the doors of the new convent, but she also had a statue of St. Ann with the Virgin and Christ Child on the stairway, and in her cell she kept a statuette of Mary, besides sending one to one of her brothers in South America. To honor the Mother of God still further, Teresa dedicated one of the little hermitage huts in the convent garden to Our Lady of Nazareth, and later she insisted, despite discouraging obsta-cles, on founding several other communities on the Feast of the Assumption. She attributed an unexpected permis-sion for the Friars' first reform to Mary's intercession, and she named their first little monastery the Conception of Our Lady of Carmel. And it is noteworthy that this Saint who traveled over the rough and mountainous roads of cen-tral Spain for twenty years in heat or rain or snow, in carts or on mules, once compassionately urged a noble lady before a trip to recall the sufferings of Mary on her journeys.

"It is very wonderful," wrote Teresa, "how pleasing to Our Lord is any service whatever done to His Mother, and His mercy is great!" And in fact, Christ revealed to the Saint that the salvation of a certain worldly young man, whom she knew, had been in serious danger—he had died without the Sacraments—but that God had had compassion on him because of the good deed which he had performed for Mary in giving his house to her Carmelite Friars for a monastery.

As Teresa's trials increased, Our Lord encouraged His faith-ful servant with these words: "Be strong, for thou seest how

ST. TERESA OF AVILA is pictured here at age 60 in a painting by Fray Juan de la Miseria. The Saint's writings reveal that the Blessed Virgin helped her many times and bestowed mystical favors upon her.
Right: An antique statue of Our Lady and the Child Jesus. The alabaster statue is venerated in the Carmelite convent of Valladolid, Spain, founded by St. Teresa in 1568.

I rely on thee. Thou shalt see the Order of the Virgin greatly advanced in thy days."

When St. Teresa was made Prioress of a large unreformed convent in which she was welcomed with shrieks of insult and hatred, at the first chapter meeting—with her typical humility and charm—she placed an image of Our Lady of Mercy in the Prioress' seat, with the keys of the convent in her hand, while Teresa sat modestly at Mary's feet. Within a few months her enemies were won over by her unique combination of saintly charity, practical ability and contagious good humor. Yet she gave all the credit for the amazing change to Mary, saying with her charming smile: "My Prioress accomplishes these wonders!"

And as a divine proof that the Blessed Virgin was indeed the Heavenly Prioress of the convent, one evening during choir, "at the beginning of the *Salve* I saw the Mother of God descend with a multitude of angels to the stall of the Prioress, where the image of Our Lady is, and sit there herself. . . She remained there during the *Salve* and said to me: 'You have done well to place me here. I will be present when the Sisters sing the praises of my Son and I will offer them to Him.' After this I remained in prayer. . .and it seemed to me that the Person of the Father drew me to Himself and spoke most comforting words to me. Among them were these, while showing how He loved me: 'I give you My Son and the Holy Ghost and the Virgin. What can you give Me?'"

Once the Saint had "a special joy on the Feast of Our Lady's Nativity. When this day came, I thought it would be well to renew our vows, and then I saw Our Lady. . .and it seemed to me as if we made them before her and that they were pleasing to her. I had this vision constantly for some days, and Our Lady was beside me on my left hand."

During the last years of her eventful life, as Our Lord drew the Saint to Himself along the Way of the Cross, Teresa suffered increasing opposition and even cruel persecution. Yet when her enemies denounced her to the Inquisition as a heretic, Mary said to her: "Do not grieve, for this cause is mine." And the Saint had good reason to write that Our Lady "is accustomed to help those who wish to place themselves under her protection." For when the formal abolition of Teresa's reformed communities seemed both imminent and inevitable, after she had been so broken-hearted that she had wept all through the day before Christmas and the Midnight Mass, finally, on the vigil of the Feast of her beloved Patron, St. Joseph, while she "was at prayer. . .she saw him in a vision with the Virgin, praying to her Son for the reform." At Christ's order she had written directly to King Philip II: "I am quite convinced that Our Lady has desired to avail herself of Your Majesty and to take you as defender for the relief of her Order. . ." Now, within a few weeks, the highest authorities of Church and State approved and recognized her reform movement as the independent Order of Discalced Carmelite nuns and friars.

After an equally painful mystical experience St. Teresa wrote, "Now I understand more of that piercing which Our Lady suffered. I saw Our Lord very distinctly close beside me and He began to comfort me with great kindness and said to me: 'Behold My Wounds. Thou art not without Me. Finish the short course of thy life.' He said to me that when He rose again He showed Himself to Our Lady, because she was in great anguish. . .He remained long with her in order to console her."

And one night toward the end of Teresa's life, "At Matins Our Lord laid Himself in my arms as He is painted in the pictures of the Sorrowful Mother. . .He said to me: 'Be not afraid, for the union of My Father with thy soul is incomparably closer than this.'"

Most fittingly, Mary's apostolic reformer, after having founded numerous self-multiplying communities of contemplative saints living joyfully in holy poverty and love of God, died peacefully on the Feast of St. Francis in the year 1582.

CHAPTER SIXTEEN

ST. JOHN OF THE CROSS
(1542-1591)

FOR THE IMPORTANT task of instituting a reform among the Spanish Carmelite Friars, the Glorious Virgin of Mount Carmel selected a valiant little mystical poet named John of the Cross. And as though to prove to the world how highly she valued his services to her Order, the merciful Mother of God appeared to him and miraculously saved his life, not just once or twice, but *five* times.

The great St. Teresa of Avila declared, with the insight of an expert, that her dear friend and fellow reformer John of the Cross had been "a saint all his life." And in fact even as a child he had practiced penances. From the age of seven he slept on a heap of twigs. He was devout, thoughtful — and poor. After his father's death, he had to beg in the streets of Medina del Campo for food to support his good mother, who taught him to pray to Mary, the Heavenly Mother of the poor and the Help of Christians. One day while playing, the five-year-old John fell into a deep, muddy pool. He was drowning when he saw a beautiful, resplendent Lady above him, and she said to him affectionately: "Give me your hand, child, and I will draw you out."

But John could not bring himself to touch the Lady's spotless and lovely hands, for fear of soiling them. A peasant who was passing by at that moment managed to pull the boy out of the pool by holding out a stick to him. All his life John was convinced that the Blessed Virgin had saved him, and he used to make fun of himself for having refused to give her his hand. He soon became "exceedingly devoted to Our Lady," and later he never failed to make a pilgrimage to that spot whenever he was in the neighborhood, in order to thank Mary for saving his life and to renew his consecration of himself to her.

At the age of twelve John became an assistant male nurse in the public hospital, while at the same time going to school. Once when on his way from school to the hospital, he fell into a well, but rescuers saw him floating calmly on the surface of the water. When they drew him up by means of a rope, he explained that as he was falling a lovely Lady had caught him in her arms and held him up until he grasped the rope.

"His fervent love for the Immaculate Virgin Mary, Mother of God, increased daily," and he longed to lead a life of silent prayer and contemplation like hers. While praying to God for guidance in the choice of a vocation, he heard Our Lord say to him: "You shall serve Me in an Order that you will bring back to its ancient perfection."

After much prayer and reflection, John decided to join the Order of the Virgin of Carmel, since it had been established for the honor and service of Mary. So on February 24, 1563, he was given the white mantle of the Carmelite Friars, which they had adopted in order that "the candor and purity of Our Lady might appear in them."

As a novice, John heard about the marvelous apparition of the merciful Mother of God to the English Carmelite, St. Simon Stock, in 1251, when she had given to the world her Scapular and her promise of salvation for all those (enrolled in the Scapular) who died wearing it. Now, too, he was initiated into the beautiful Marian liturgy of the Carmelite Order, of which it has been written that "the whole day was set in songs of praise to Mary." Throughout John's life, "on feasts of the Blessed Virgin his love for the Mother of God was evident" in his appearance and countenance.

The following year, he went to study for the priesthood at the University of Salamanca, where he became acquainted with a holy Portuguese friar who expressed his love for Mary so fervently and so eloquently that when he died, his tongue remained incorrupt.

John was ordained a priest at the age of twenty-five, in September, 1567, and he celebrated his first Holy Mass at Medina del Campo, in the presence of his mother and brother, during the Octave of Our Lady's Nativity. At the Consecration, the young Saint begged his Eucharistic Lord to grant him the grace never to offend Him by mortal sin and to suffer during his life the penance for all the faults which he might have committed if God were not sustaining him with His grace. It was later revealed to a holy nun that John's prayer was immediately answered, that he was re-established in the purity and innocence of a two-year-old child, and that he was especially strengthened in grace like the Apostles.

Now John longed more than ever to live a life of solitude and contemplation. He therefore decided to leave the Carmelite Order and become a Carthusian. But Our Lady of Mount Carmel had other plans for her valiant little mystic.

Soon he was introduced to St. Teresa of Avila. And when he told her of his growing urge "to separate himself from the world and hide himself in God," she revealed to him her very practical plans for the revival of the ancient contemplative life of the Order of the Blessed Virgin. "I made him see," she wrote, "that if he wished to embrace a more perfect life, it would be better to do so in his own Order." At last, with her help, John understood the puzzling prophecy which Jesus had made concerning his destiny.

Soon after meeting the holy little friar, Teresa noted in a letter: "He is indeed small in stature"—he was only five feet, two inches tall—"but in my opinion he is very great in the sight of God. I find him most fitted for our kind of life. I really do believe that God is calling him to this undertaking. He is still young"—he was twenty-five, while she was in her early fifties—"but he has always practiced the most severe penance." Later, when she knew him still better, she wrote: "I have found a man according to the heart of God and my own. I seek here and there for light and find all I need in my little (John). He is really the father of my soul and one of those who have done me most good...He has reached as great a degree of sanctity as a creature can reach in this life." And Our Lord Himself revealed to her that John could "travel the same road as you."

This road was one that inevitably led to Calvary. Within ten years, after St. Teresa and St. John had founded several monasteries of Reformed or Discalced Carmelite Friars, a bitter conflict between these and the Calced Fathers, largely due to a complicated maze of contradictory jurisdictions among various ecclesiastical authorities, reached a point at which the opponents of the Reform decided to abolish it by force.

On December 3, 1577, St. John of the Cross, who was then serving as confessor to the Carmelite nuns in Avila, was taken prisoner by his enemies, scourged twice, and sent to the large monastery of Toledo, where he was locked up in a tiny, dark cell.

At first every evening, then three times a week, and finally only on Fridays, he was conducted to the refectory and forced to sit on the floor while eating his meal of bread and water. Then he would bare his shoulders and the friars would file by and scourge him with whips that left scars still visible fourteen years later. However, knowing that they sincerely considered him a proud rebel against legal authority, the Saint willingly forgave them, prayed for them and later would not allow anyone to criticize them. His keen mental anguish was increased, not by the honors with which his enemies tried to bribe him, but by the fear that the Reform might already have failed.

For eight long months, during which he was not allowed to change his habit, he endured a physical and spiritual "Dark Night of the Spirit" in which his valiant soul was utterly purified and mystically united to the bleeding Heart of his Crucified Saviour. It was during these eight months of suffering "in body and soul" that John composed some of his most beautiful poems. Twice at night his jailer and several friars saw a bright light shining through the cracks of his cell's door, but it vanished when they entered. It is believed that Jesus and Mary visited him several times.

On August 14, 1578, when asked what he was thinking, John said to the Prior: "I was thinking that tomorrow is the Feast of Our Lady, and it would be a great consolation for me if I could say Mass..."

"Not in my time!" replied the Prior mercilessly.

But on the night of her great feast day, the merciful Mother of God appeared to the valiant mystic in all her radiant beauty and glory and said to him, "Have patience, my son, for your trials will soon cease. You shall leave this prison, say Mass and be consoled."

And a few days later, Mary showed him in a vision a window high up on the monastery wall and told him that he was to escape by it with her help. She also assisted him in loosening the double locks of his prison. Then, one night, despite the fact that two friars were sleeping in the room outside his cell, after praying fervently to Our Lady, John made his way through the dark monastery to the right window and let himself down by a rope which he had made with two coverlets and a tunic. He had to drop nine feet onto the city wall and then into a convent garden. Suddenly he saw a bright light and heard a voice say, "Follow me." He went to a high wall and leaned against it, despairing of being strong enough to climb over it...But a moment later he somehow found himself standing in a narrow street on the other side of the wall—free—as the Blessed Mother had promised!

Thereafter, whenever he felt tired or sad, St. John of the Cross would refresh himself simply by thinking of the Blessed Virgin or by singing a hymn in her honor, and he would always recite her Office on his knees. He used to speak of her with the greatest tenderness and affection, and he would endeavor to inspire devotion toward her in his friars by telling them that the innumerable favors which she had bestowed on him were such that the mere sight of her image gave him new life and filled his soul with love and joy. In fact, he kept a picture of the Mother of God in his bare cell.

John happened to be in his cell one day when some construction workers caused a whole wall of the monastery to fall in the wrong direction—onto his cell. Everyone believed that he had been crushed to death. Nevertheless they frantically cleared away the debris, and to their amazement they found the little Saint standing in a corner of his cell, unharmed and smiling. When he was asked how he could have escaped injury, he replied simply: "She of the white mantle covered me with it."

On another occasion, when John was delayed at a ford by a dangerous flood, he heard an inner voice urging him to continue his journey, and so he went into the swollen torrent on his mule. But in midstream the animal's feet became entangled in some driftwood, and both mule and rider sank beneath the rushing water. As usual, John prayed fervently to Our Lady—and soon he and his mule were seen on the opposite bank. Then he hastened on the road to an inn—which he reached just in time to hear the last Confession of a man dying from wounds received in a quarrel.

Like the Seraphic Francis of Assisi, whom he very much resembled, Mary's valiant little Spanish mystic, reformer and poet was also one of the most charming and lovable saints in history, not only towards his friars and nuns, but especially with the many lay persons who came to him for Confession or advice. He was constantly performing small or

ON FIVE OCCASIONS the life of St. John of the Cross (1542-1591) was miraculously saved by the merciful Mother of God. The Spanish Saint worked with St. Teresa of Avila in the great Reform of the Carmelite Order. He is also held to be one of the most charming and lovable Saints in the history of the Church.

Schamoni

VALIANT MYSTIC St. John of the Cross underwent great sufferings in his life as a Discalced Carmelite. These bore fruit for future generations through his great spiritual classics, including *The Dark Night of the Soul.* St. John of the Cross is a Doctor of the Church and is known as "The Mystical Doctor."

heroic acts of kindness and thoughtfulness for those around him. And far from being a cold, strict and forbidding "kill-joy," because he was utterly detached from all selfish or worldly pleasures, John of the Cross was overflowing with true supernatural joy and warmth and love for the beauties of God's nature, as well as with touching compassion for the purifying sufferings of his fellow men. Few saints have been loved so intensely as he was by his numerous friends and disciples.

Because "he wrote from the experimental knowledge which he had lived," his four famous mystical treatises, *The Ascent of Mount Carmel, The Dark Night of the Soul, The Spiritual Canticle* and *The Living Flame of Love,* have earned for him in our times the rare honor of being named Doctor of the Church. But the soul of the Saint is more easily grasped in his striking brief sayings, of which we can quote only a few:

"First of all, have a constant care and desire of imitating Christ in everything, conforming yourself to His life, which you must study well in order to know how to follow it." "Where there is no love, put in love and you will draw love out." "Compassion for one's neighbor increases in proportion as the soul is united to God by love." "A very little of this pure love is more precious in the sight of God and of greater profit to the Church—even though the soul appears to be doing nothing—than are all other works put together." "Up, little children, let us get on the road to Life Eternal!" "The apostolic life is a life of contempt." "To suffer—to act—to be silent!"

One day toward the end of his life, while in prayer before a certain crucifix, the Saint heard Jesus say to him, "Brother John, ask Me for what you wish, and I will give it to you, for the services which you have done for Me."

And St. John of the Cross replied, "Lord, what I wish You to give me is suffering to be borne for Your sake, and that I may be despised and regarded as worthless."

And when he knew that he would soon be leaving this world, John prayed that God might grant him these three

favors: "Not to die as a superior, to die where he was not
even known, and to die after having suffered a great deal."
His prayers were fully answered.

In the summer of 1591, when the Saint was only forty-
nine years old, he was unjustly persecuted and deprived
of all his offices in his own Order and sent in disgrace and
exile to a remote hermitage. Soon he became seriously ill
and for three months suffered intensely from numerous
festering ulcers in his legs, back and shoulders. Finally, on
the Vigil of the Feast of the Immaculate Conception, it was
revealed to him that he was going to die on the following
Saturday, the Octave of Mary's great Feast, and he joyfully
recalled the Scapular Promise of Our Lady of Carmel "that
she comes on Saturdays to Purgatory and withdraws from
it the souls of devout persons who have worn her holy Scapular." Then the Saint was heard to exclaim: "Blessed be the
Lady who intends me to leave this life on a Saturday!"

At ten o'clock on the next Friday night, when he was told
that the friars were going to choir for Matins, John said:
"And I, by the mercy of my God, am going to recite them
with the Virgin, Our Lady, in Heaven. . .at midnight!"

Precisely at midnight, while the monastery bell was ringing, an extremely bright supernatural light filled the cell
of Our Lady's valiant mystic, and little Father John of the
Cross went to Heaven, to his beloved God, to pray and intercede for mankind until the end of the world—"with the Virgin, Our Lady."

CHAPTER SEVENTEEN

ST. CATHERINE LABOURÉ
(1806-1876)

O N JULY 27, 1947, Our Holy Father Pius XII solemnly
canonized the humble and still little-known French
nun through whom the Blessed Virgin had given her Miraculous Medal to the world in 1830, thereby inaugurating the
marvelous series of great modern Marian apparitions that
would seem to be a prelude to the "Age of Mary" of which
the holy Marian apostle St. Louis Marie Grignion De Montfort wrote over two hundred years ago: "It is by the Blessed
Virgin Mary that Jesus Christ came into the world; it is also
by her that He is to reign in the world. This reign will
be a necessary consequence of the knowledge and reign
of the Blessed Virgin. She will produce by the power of
the Holy Spirit the greatest prodigies in those latter times.
May the reign of Mary come, that Thy reign, O Jesus, may
come!"

And St. Catherine Labouré prophesied that a time would
come when all mankind would honor Mary as "Queen of
the World."

In 1830, at the time of the epoch-making Miraculous Medal Apparitions, Catherine Labouré was a simple and devout French peasant girl of twenty-four who had been in the novices' convent of the Daughters of Charity in Paris for only three months. As far as anyone could see then or throughout the rest of her life, there was nothing remarkable about this tall, reserved, model nun, for she always kept the secrets of her rich inner life to herself.

Her greatest secret was her intense and fervent love for the Blessed Virgin. Catherine's devout mother had often told her: "In our sorrows we must always run to Mary—she never turns away from a child who loves her!" And one day, after that good peasant mother had died, a servant saw little Catherine standing on the living room table with her arms stretched out toward a statue of the Mother of God and of men. Then, reaching up, the child tenderly gave Mary a long kiss. . .

Ever since her First Holy Communion, Catherine had wanted to become a nun. And at the age of eighteen she had a strange dream: after attending a Mass said by a saintly old priest, she met him while visiting a sick person, and he said to her: "My daughter, it is good to nurse the sick. Now you avoid me, but one day you will be very glad to come to me. The Good Lord has plans for you—do not forget it!" Later, in a convent of the Daughters of Charity, she immediately recognized the old priest in a picture of their founder, St. Vincent de Paul.

Now, on the night of July 18, 1830, the eve of the Feast of St. Vincent de Paul, young Sister Catherine retired to her curtained cubicle in the convent dormitory with a very special prayer in her heart. We will let the Saint herself tell us in her own beautifully simple words (slightly condensed) exactly what happened to her then:

"I went to bed with the thought that this night I would see my Good Mother. I had been wanting to see her for so long! At last I fell asleep with the thought that St. Vincent would obtain for me the grace of seeing the Blessed Virgin.

"At last, at half-past eleven at night, I heard myself being called by my name. Waking up, I drew back the curtain and saw a child dressed in white, about four or five years old, who said to me: 'Come to the chapel. Get right up and come to the chapel. The Blessed Virgin is waiting for you!'

"I hastened to get dressed and followed the child. The lights were lit wherever we passed, which greatly astonished me. But I was much more surprised when I entered the chapel. I saw all the candles and lights lit, which reminded me of midnight Mass. However, I did not see the Blessed Virgin. The child led me into the sanctuary near the direc-tor's chair, and there I knelt down, and the child remained standing. As I found the time dragging, I looked around. . .Finally the child warned me. He said to me: 'Here is the Blessed Virgin—here she is!'

"I heard a noise like the rustling of a silk dress which came from near the picture of St. Joseph and which went and stopped by the altar steps at the Gospel side in the chair. At that moment it would be impossible for me to say what I felt. Then, looking at the Blessed Virgin, I sprang forward with one leap to her side—kneeling on the altar steps with my hands resting on the knees of the Blessed Virgin. There I spent the sweetest moment in my life. It would be impossible for me to tell all that I have experienced. She told me how I should act with my director and several things which I must not tell, how to act in my sufferings ahead, and, showing me the foot of the altar with her left hand, she told me to come and pour out my heart there; I would receive all the consolations I would need. Then she said to me:

" 'My child, the good God wishes to charge you with a mission. You will suffer many trials on account of it, but you will overcome them with the thought that it is for the glory of God. You will be contradicted, but you will have grace—do not fear. You will see certain things. You will be inspired in your prayers. Give (your confessor) an account of them.'

"Then I asked her the meaning of all the things which I had seen, and she explained it all:

"'My child, times are very bad. Calamities are going to fall upon France. *The whole world will be in an upheaval due to all sorts of troubles.*'" The Blessed Virgin was very sad when she said this.

"'But come to the foot of this altar. There, graces will be shed upon all those who ask for them with confidence and fervor. . . A moment will come when danger will be great. It will seem as if all were lost. But have confidence — I will be with you. . . My child, the Cross will be scorned. It will be thrown to the ground. They will again open the side of Our Lord. The streets will be filled with blood. *The whole world will be in sorrow.*'"

At this point Mary could no longer speak. Her features expressed profound grief.

"I do not know how long I stayed there. When she left, I only perceived something that was being extinguished, finally just a shadow, going the same way she had come. I got up and saw the child. He said to me: 'She is gone.'

"We went back the same way. I think that child was my Guardian Angel. When I was back in bed, it was two o'clock in the morning. I heard it ring. I did not go back to sleep."

Within a few days Catherine told her confessor, Father Aladel, all about the vision, but he prudently paid little attention to it.

Four months later, at five-thirty on the afternoon of November 27, 1830, during a community meditation period in the chapel, Catherine again saw the Mother of God, dressed in white and standing on a globe. At first Mary was holding a small globe, above which was a little golden cross. She was looking up toward Heaven, and her countenance was radiant as she offered the world to Our Lord. She was indescribably beautiful. She seemed to press and warm the globe in her hands and against her Immaculate Heart, while offering it to her Divine Son with an expression of ineffable love and supplication, as Advocate and Mother of all mankind.

Then, after this act of intercession, all of a sudden Mary's hands blazed with dazzling light. Her fingers were covered with sparkling and gleaming jewels which sent forth bright rays of light that fell onto the great globe at her feet as she lowered her hands. Now she looked down at Catherine, and the Saint heard a voice say to her: "This globe which you see represents the world as a whole and France in particular and each separate individual." Then, referring to the streams of light: "This is the symbol of the graces which I shed on those who ask me for them." And Catherine adds: "She made me understand how pleasing it was to pray to the Blessed Virgin, and how generous she was toward persons who pray to her, what joy she gives them. At that moment I was beyond myself with bliss.

"A slightly oval frame formed around the Blessed Virgin, and over it were these words: 'O MARY CONCEIVED WITHOUT SIN, PRAY FOR US WHO HAVE RECOURSE TO THEE,' written in letters of gold. Then I heard a voice that said to me: *Have a medal made according to this model. Everybody who wears it will receive great graces by wearing it around the neck. The graces will be abundant for persons who wear it with confidence.*'" And Catherine was also shown the reverse side of the medal, with the Cross, the "M," the two Hearts and the twelve Stars.

But again Father Aladel dismissed the apparition with the wise advice that the best way to please Our Lady was to imitate her virtues.

Finally, in December, 1830, the Saint had a last vision of the Blessed Virgin, standing above and in the rear of the tabernacle on the altar. This time she also saw under Mary's feet a greenish serpent with yellow spots. Noticing that some of the jewels on her hands did not sparkle, Catherine was told: "Those stones which remain dark symbolize the graces that people have forgotten to request." Again she was shown the designs for the Medals and ordered to have them made. And before leaving her, Mary said:

"My daughter, henceforth you will no longer see me. But

you will hear my voice in your prayers."

Then the beautiful vision vanished. And Catherine recalled: "I remained filled with — I don't know what — with good feelings, and with joy and consolation!"

Father Aladel, though increasingly stirred interiorly, still refused to commit himself. Meanwhile, Catherine was assigned to washing the dishes in the Daughters of Charity's home for the aged in Paris. One day she said to Mary in prayer: "My Good Mother, you see clearly that Father Aladel does not believe me. He does not want to have your Medal made."

"Don't worry," replied the Blessed Virgin. "A day will come when he will do what I want. He is my servant. He would be afraid of displeasing me."

And at last, in 1832, the good priest had some of the medals made and distributed, with the approval of the Archbishop of Paris. Within only two years Mary's little medal became known as the Miraculous Medal, so numerous and so sensational were the cures and conversions which she brought about as it spread like wildfire all over Europe. By 1836, over six million medals had been made in Paris and Lyons alone, to say nothing of the twelve other cities in which they were also being manufactured by the millions. Furthermore, the Medal's motto greatly increased popular devotion to Mary's Immaculate Conception, which was duly defined as a dogma in 1854.

Sister Catherine also revealed to Father Aladel that the Blessed Virgin wished him to found and to direct the Sodality of the Children of Mary. And through her anonymous Saint (no one but Father Aladel knew that Catherine was "the sister of the Apparitions"), the Mother of God gave this lovely prayer to all children who consecrated themselves to her:

"O Mary Immaculate, cover me with your virginal mantle, that I may come forth from it purified, and present me to Jesus, your beloved Son.

"O Mary Immaculate, the most pure, the most holy, and the most perfect of creatures, lead all your children to Heaven!"

ST. CATHERINE LABOURÉ (1806-1876), a French Daughter of Charity, was selected by the Blessed Mother to give the Miraculous Medal to the world. The Saint prophesied that all mankind would someday honor Our Lady as "Queen of the World."

Courtesy, St. Joseph's Provincial House Archives

THE BLESSED VIRGIN told St. Catherine Labouré, ". . . My child, the good God wishes to charge you with a mission. You will suffer many trials on account of it, but you will overcome them with the thought that it is for the glory of God."

St. Catherine Labouré predicted to her confessor that in the future, the month of Mary would be celebrated throughout the Church with much magnificence, and that devotion to the Sacred Heart and to St. Joseph would greatly increase. Speaking of those days to come, she exclaimed: *"Oh, how beautiful it will be to hear people say: 'MARY IS THE QUEEN OF THE WORLD!' She will be honored with banners, and she will go all around the world."*

And yet for forty-six long years Mary's humble anonymous Saint kept her precious secret, while living the hidden life of an unknown and unnoticed Daughter of Charity in charge of the old men's ward and the poultry yard of the community's hospital in Paris. Though Father Aladel did tell the Sisters that it was one of them who had received the famous medal, no one knew that it was the very plain and quite ordinary Sister Labouré. And when Father Aladel died, the secret went to the grave with him. Catherine's Mother Superior said later, after finally learning from Catherine that she was the favored seer: "Despite the whispered assurances that she was the Sister so favored by the Blessed Virgin, I scarcely credited it, so much was her life like that of others." However, "We were always struck when saying the Rosary together by the serious and devout way in which our dear companion said the Hail Mary. She who was always so humble and so reserved could not refrain from condemning the indifference and lack of attention that too often accompany the recitation of this prayer." Some of the nuns also remarked that while praying, Sister Catherine always gazed at a statue of Mary, and that on all feasts of the Blessed Virgin she was either sick or suffering acute pain. On one Feast of the Immaculate Conception she slipped and fell while stepping into a bus and broke her wrist. Without saying a word to her companion, the Saint simply clasped her wrist with her other hand, and when asked what she was holding, she replied quietly: "Sister, I am holding my bouquet—every year the Blessed Virgin sends me one this way."

Early in 1876 Catherine Labouré informed her Sisters that she would be gone within a year, and with Mary's permission she gave a full account of the Apparitions to her Mother Superior. On her deathbed, just before peacefully leaving this world on December 31, 1876, Catherine said, "The Blessed Virgin has promised to grant special graces every time someone prays in the Chapel, but especially an increase of purity—that purity of mind, heart and will which is pure love..."

And seventy years later, by a significant design of God's Providence, Holy Mother Church canonized, within the space of eight days, both the holy priest (St. Louis De Montfort) who had foreseen the Age of Mary and the humble nun who may have inaugurated it!

THE INCORRUPT BODY of St. Catherine Labouré, which rests in the chapel of the Daughters of Charity in rue du Bac, Paris.

✠ SAINT BENEDICT✝PRESS

Saint Benedict Press, founded in 2006, is the parent company for a variety of imprints including TAN Books, Catholic Courses, Benedict Bibles, Benedict Books, and Labora Books. The company's name pays homage to the guiding influence of the Rule of Saint Benedict and the Benedictine monks of Belmont Abbey, North Carolina, just a short distance from the company's headquarters in Charlotte, NC.

Saint Benedict Press is now a multi-media company. Its mission is to publish and distribute products reflective of the Catholic intellectual tradition and to present these products in an attractive and accessible manner.

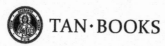

TAN·BOOKS

TAN Books was founded in 1967, in response to the rapid decline of faith and morals in society and the Church. Since its founding, TAN Books has been committed to the preservation and promotion of the spiritual, theological and liturgical traditions of the Catholic Church. In 2008, TAN Books was acquired by Saint Benedict Press. Since then, TAN has experienced positive growth and diversification while fulfilling its mission to a new generation of readers.

TAN Books publishes over 500 titles on Thomistic theology, traditional devotions, Church doctrine, history, lives of the saints, educational resources, and booklets.

For a free catalog from Saint Benedict Press
or TAN Books, visit us online at
saintbenedictpress.com • tanbooks.com
or call us toll-free at
(800) 437-5876